Massive Charisma:
Likability, Charm, Presence, and Success With People

By Patrick King
Social Interaction and Conversation Coach at
www.PatrickKingConsulting.com

Table of Contents

Part 1: Cultivating a Charismatic Aura

Chapter 1: So, what is charisma anyway?

There's something about them. People with charisma are just so... *appealing*. They're charming, they're likable and they somehow make everyone gravitate towards them. Is it magic? Is it just a chemistry thing?

If you've ever wanted to be that person in the room with the most magnetic, captivating aura, then this book is for you. When we're in the presence of charismatic people, it can be hard to say precisely why we're so bewitched. Charisma can start to seem like something that you're just born with... or not.

But thankfully, this kind of allure is *not* some mysterious power that only a few possess. It's 100% a social skill that you can practice, even if you don't quite see yourself that way now.

Charisma is really a collection of different behaviors and attitudes that radiate a certain very attractive mindset to others. We'll divide our "charisma crash course" into two main parts in the chapters that follow. First, you'll learn how to develop your own unique brand of charm within yourself. Then, in part 2, you'll learn to carry that aura out into the world and broadcast it to those you interact with.

With charisma, you're more empathetic, more engaging, and a much, much better conversationalist. You're interesting *and* interested. And because you're witty and emotionally intelligent, people like you and trust you. It's hard to imagine an area of life that isn't improved with a little charisma – dating, work, friendships. Even chatting to strangers at a bus stop becomes an opportunity for winning people over with enchanting banter!

Before we dive in, though, let's dispel one misconception: being charismatic is NOT about being loud, extroverted or cocky. In fact, by the end of this book, the hope is that you'll see there are many ways to be charming, whether that's being flashy and larger than life, or quietly confident and a little mysterious.

A practical definition

Conveniently for us, in 2018, researchers at the University of Toronto studied the phenomena of charisma and developed a working definition. After studying over 1000 people, the team concluded that charisma was a mix of two things:

1. Affability
2. Influence

Affability broadly means that people are pleasant to be around and easily approachable. However you define it – warmth, pleasantness, friendliness – this is the quality that makes you think, "hm, I like this person!"

Influence is defined as leadership potential, "presence" and the ability to influence and persuade people. Not only did the team discover that it was actually possible to measure these two traits, but also that people were fairly accurate at rating themselves – i.e. when self-ratings were compared to ratings by others, they were more or less the same. They created the General Charisma Inventory (GCI), which you can basically complete yourself right now:

Read the following statements and give yourself a rating from 1 to 5, with 1 for "strongly disagree" and 5 for "strongly agree." The first three are about influence, while the latter three are about affability.

I am someone who...

- *Has a presence in a room*
- *Has the ability to influence people*
- *Knows how to lead a group*
- *Makes people feel comfortable*
- *Smiles at people often*
- *Can get along with anyone*

To score, simply add up the ratings for each, and take that value and divide it by 6. If you scored over 3.7, you can consider your charisma above average. Scored significantly lower than that? Don't worry! It's not as hard as you might think to work on these 6 criteria and boost your charm. Did you score low in influence, affability or both? Interestingly, how charismatic you are has nothing to do with your personality type or overall intelligence (it may have something to do with whether you're male or female, though – more on that later).

So, let's summarize: charisma is characterized by the ability to charm, persuade and attract others, and it contains two broad traits, *affability* and the power to *influence*. These two broad traits can be broken down into 6 smaller characteristics, such as presence and good rapport with others. Let's take a closer look at the basic dos and don'ts of charisma.

Being more influential

Think of a person you consider influential. What are they like? Maybe you picture someone like Oprah Winfrey, who built a veritable empire for herself, and influenced millions of people worldwide. Or maybe you picture Mahatma Gandhi, whose non-violent resistance created an aura of decisiveness so powerful it influenced nations. Whoever you think of when you hear "influential," that person is probably one thing: confident.

Influential people believe in themselves and communicate the things they're passionate about, so much so that other people feel passionate and confident about those things, too! Think of the most famous political speeches in history and how their speakers could transmit their energy and enthusiasm to the crowd. It's not ever about arrogance or narcissism, though. Instead, it's about that person's *presence*.

Picture someone walking into a room, head held high, smile on their face, body language open. They greet everyone in the room confidently, and when they speak, their voice is sure, crisp and clear. Immediately, they seem to take up a certain amount of space in the room. Compare this to someone who slinks in shyly, shoulders slumped, expression of apprehension all over their face. Without making eye contact, they greet one person and then shuffle off to a corner somewhere, speaking quietly, if at all. It's obvious: this person simply takes up less room.

However, taking up more "space" is not just about being literally larger than life. People try to cheat with this and wear outrageous, attention-grabbing clothing or speak too loudly – this will catch people's attention for a second, but is unlikely to hold it if there is no genuine confidence and gravity in your presence beyond the costume!

DO THIS: Before you walk into a room or start a conversation, literally stand tall and stretch your arms high over your head. Take deep breaths. Imagine a light at the center of your chest. This light is who you are, the best of you, and what you have to offer the world. Imagine proudly and courageously shining this light out when you move around the world, with open body language and a smile.

One way to immediately get into this open, optimistic posture is to imagine that the people you're about to encounter are *already* your friends, and that you will be received warmly. Imagine that you're meeting old, much-loved friends who are dying to see you. Carry that unguarded expectation and optimism into any new interaction.

DON'T DO THIS: If you have a core belief that certain people or situations are threatening, then this attitude will manifest in your expression, your posture and your voice. You will transmit an attitude (no matter how subtle or unconscious) or fearfulness, reluctance or hostility – and that will immediately destroy any chance of charisma. So, whatever you do, *don't* enter into any interaction where you're quietly thinking, "these people hate me." This attitude will make you shrivel, shrink and fold into yourself, immediately taking up less space and losing presence in the room.

What about influencing others? Presence is one thing, but to encourage others to think or do certain things, you'll need to have one important thing: energy. You have to not only believe in yourself (confidence, taking up space) but believe in what you're saying. If you can genuinely muster enthusiasm and optimism for your point of view, people will be more attracted to it. If you're non-committal? Others will respond in the same lukewarm way, if they pay attention at all.

DO THIS: Find your real passion, and speak fervently about it. You can't fake enthusiasm. People can tell when they're being manipulated or advertised to – but they love it when others are fired up with their own mission, and are following their own north star. They love that enthusiasm so much they want to follow that north star, too! Whether you're trying to get people to do something or not, speak out about what matters to you (even if you will actually "lose" some people in the process!).

Passionate about animal rights? About good food? A sport? Have you always been zealous about a particular hobby, interest or view? Then say so! At the very least, be bold and confident in stating what you like and want. Don't sit on the fence. Do you have an unusual preference or opinion? Share it proudly, without diluting your true feelings.

DON'T DO THIS: "Uh, I don't know, what do *you* think?" Not very inspiring, right? Banish these words from your vocabulary. Even though you might feel that way inside, don't second guess or self-doubt out loud. Charismatic people are relaxed, confident and sure of themselves. So, if you portray anxiety, uncertainty or doubt in the value of your ideas, you can expect others to do the same.

Also, make a point of not complaining, whining or expressing dissatisfaction about yourself. It's the opposite of inspiring passion. Here's a secret: people don't really mind if others are wrong or different, so long as they are confidently, authentically so!

Finally, what about leadership? If you are confident and can speak clearly about your passions, then you will automatically find yourself in the position of leading others. The good news is that there is really no such thing as a "natural" leader – if you have a compelling and genuine vision, and you communicate that well to others, they will be inspired to follow.

DO THIS: Speak TO people and not AT them. What do they value? What do they want? How do they make sense of the world? Speak to your audience's highest selves. When you talk to them, communicate so that you *center their perspective,* rather than your own. Make your vision so real for them they can taste it.

For example, if you're part of a committee and you're trying to get people to see the wisdom of a new plan you're proposing, you might listen to the way they speak and reflect that back to them, using their words and not your own. You might adjust how you speak to frame the plan to align with their values and principles. "I know that you're a family man, and you're as concerned as I am about child safeguarding."

DON'T DO THIS: Treat people as objects to be moved. Force and manipulation might work in the very short term but ultimately fail. You may have a brilliant idea, but if you force it on others with no respect for them, they won't listen. Avoid appealing to your audience's lowest selves – the part of them that responds from fear or hate or negativity. This will not be felt as influence, but manipulation. "Well, you have kids. Wouldn't you feel really guilty if you let something bad happen to them?"

Being more affable

Many politicians are quite influential... but nobody *likes* them. Influence is only half of charisma – people need to like you. Many people who struggle with socializing fail to realize the most important part of being likeable: making other people feel good. It's not about getting others to think you're great; rather, it's about making sure they feel comfortable, listened to, and respected. When people feel that they are liked in this way, then, as if by magic, they like *you*.

Being more affable is easy once you get out of your own head. The easiest (almost too easy) way to be more affable is simply to smile. Smile as often as you can. Remember that people cannot see into your inner experience – they can only see what you're broadcasting on your face. So be aware of your facial muscles and what they're communicating. Check in occasionally and consciously remind yourself to loosen your jaw, unclench your forehead muscles and gently lift the corners of your mouth.

DO THIS: You don't have to grin from ear to ear constantly. But *encourage* yourself to smile more, especially if you're someone who considers themselves a little pessimistic or grumpy! You can practice genuine smiles by thinking of things that make you happy. It's a trick photographers use: they ask their models to imagine someone they love, or remember a hilarious moment. They can't help but smile or laugh. A smile doesn't have to be enormous to have an effect – as long as it's warm and genuine, it will have an effect.

Making other people feel comfortable is a big part of affability. It's easy to imagine why:

Person A: Good looking, intelligent, accomplished, fascinating, and makes you feel at ease

Person B: Good looking, intelligent, accomplished, fascinating, and makes you feel like garbage

Person A has charisma… person B is just intimidating, or even an outright bully!

Putting other people at ease takes emotional intelligence and empathy (which we'll cover at length in a later chapter). A certain degree of emotional and social maturity is required: charismatic people don't see social interactions as a chance to boast or as a battleground in which they demolish their opponents. Rather, they genuinely like other people and enjoy interacting with them. Ask yourself honestly, do you enter conversations with a genuine desire to listen to what other people say? Do you approach other people with curiosity to learn what they could teach you?

The best way to put other people at ease and make them comfortable is to pay attention to them. Listen to what they're saying (not what you think they're saying!) and show that you value and respect that perspective, rather than just barging in to share your own. You will win people's trust and admiration if you treat them with care.

DO THIS: Remember details. How do you feel when people don't spell your name right or completely forget what you told them in detail just yesterday? *Unheard*. A dazzling and interesting person who barely acknowledges your existence is not charismatic – they're more like a self-involved diva or celebrity. Instead, make a point of listening with care to what you're told. Remember facts that people tell you, and bring them up casually in later conversations. If you can do this and engage with others as though they're genuinely the most fascinating person on the planet (in that moment, they are!), then you will instantly boost your appeal.

DON'T DO THIS: Interrupt. It's something so easy and so tempting to do, and it so quickly destroys rapport. When you interrupt, you're basically telling the other person, "What I'm saying is more important than what you're saying." Obviously, this will not make them feel comfortable. Wait a few seconds after they finish speaking before you speak. Beware of more subtle forms of interrupting, too. If you continually change the topic, ignore what's been said, or deliberately steer the conversation to yourself over and over again, the effect is the same. Let go of any conversational agenda and let the other person take charge and steer things for a while.

Finally, charismatic people get along with everybody. This is important – they don't just get along with those they like or those they're similar to, but *everybody*. Two things can help you get on better with people, whoever they are: optimism and non-judgment.

Charismatic people are positive people. They're solution oriented, resilient, and look on the bright side. They see the good in themselves (self-confidence) but also the good in others. They see conversations as opportunities for learning and connection, and challenges as invitations to improve. If you are constantly negative, you bring an entirely different energy to interactions. You have an aura of difficulty, resistance, opposition, or just plain old dissatisfaction. Who would be attracted to that? If you add judgment into this mix, things are even worse.

DO THIS: Express gratitude often and openly. Something magical happens when you demonstrate appreciation, and you'll instantly come across as more positive. It can be a simple question of saying, "wow, here comes some beautiful rain! My garden is going to love all this water," instead of complaining bitterly about the lack of sunshine. Even better if you can express gratitude for the other person, instead of criticism. Rather than dwelling on how weird you find someone, say instead, "That's what I love about you, you're not like anyone else I know!"

DON'T DO THIS: Judge. That includes yourself! Avoid gossiping or complaining about others, but especially avoid talking negatively about yourself. It may seem harmless (some people even believe that a good gossip session brings people together!), but it ultimately makes you look negative and insecure. Say something constructive or at the least keep criticisms to yourself.

And there you have it – we have demystified charisma and pinned it down to six very practical, very simple skills you can try today, in your very next conversation:

1. Open up your posture and take up space; assume that people are already your friends
2. Speak up about your passions and drop self-doubting language
3. Address people's higher selves and their values to influence and win them over

4. Use happy memories to encourage yourself to smile more
5. Show people you're paying attention by remembering conversational details, and never interrupt, to put them at ease
6. Express gratitude rather than criticism and judgment, to appear more optimistic

As you can see, none of the above require any magical powers or special talents – with a little effort and practice, they can all be measured, learnt and developed.

Zooming in on personal charisma

Ronald E Riggio is the Henry R. Kravis Professor of Leadership and Organizational Psychology at Claremont McKenna College in California, and he's been studying charisma for decades, particularly when it comes to leadership. For Riggio, personal charisma is basically a complicated mix of social skills that allows people to *deeply affect others on an emotional level*, primarily using communication. It's not just that you possess a group of nifty skills, but that all the skills come together cohesively, making a deep impact on other people.

Whether on a social or emotional level, charismatic people are

1. expressive
2. sensitive to other people's expression, and
3. able to control both of these masterfully, according to the context and their own needs

Emotional awareness and *social* intelligence are key here, and with enough practice, you can bring both skills together into one big, charming package. Let's look at what Riggio calls the 6 foundational building blocks of charisma. Each is based on how well we send messages (expressiveness), receive them (sensitivity), or control ourselves.

Emotional expressiveness

You know who isn't charismatic? A robot. Stoic, restrained or emotionless people may be read as cold and unengaged. Remember our definition: charisma is about making an *emotional* impact on people. You don't do that with a list of rational arguments. You do that by expressing emotion yourself. Spontaneously and genuinely express how you feel. When you're animated and energetic, you seem more alive, more intelligent and more engrossing. When you demonstrate that you can be moved, that you have an opinion, and that you're dynamic and changeable, you appear more human and more trustworthy to others.

DO THIS: To be more expressive... use expressions. Allow your face to be animated. As you talk, imagine that all the sound is muted, or that your audience is hard of hearing, and you have to mime a little. Could an audience guess your meaning from your facial expression alone? Communicate with *all* of your body – use hand gestures and postures. Use a degree of mime and action to relate stories, change your voice to mimic someone else, and use movement to add color to anecdotes. Not sure how? Watch standup comedians with the sound off and look at how they use their bodies to express themselves.

DON'T DO THIS: Be boring in your speech. Instead, use colorful and inventive language. Be a little unexpected and fresh, describe things in unusual ways, or use unique turns of phrase. On a related note, steer clear of swearing – not because it's vulgar, but because it's uncreative! If you must be vulgar, at least find a novel way to do it...

Emotional sensitivity

Being a sophisticated communicator is not just about sending a clear message, but receiving other people's messages, too. You simply cannot connect with people emotionally if you don't even know what emotions they're experiencing. You need to be able to accurately perceive other people's emotions – and respond to what you see. This is the ability to notice when you've lost someone's attention, when they're feeling uncomfortable, or when you're connecting with them. In other words, it's empathy.

In a later chapter, we'll look more closely at exactly how to improve empathy skills, but for the time being, it's enough to know that *empathy is nothing more than a heightened ability to truly perceive another person's reality*. You only need to pay attention. Truth be told, many of us are bad at this not because it's difficult, but because we don't actually take the time to ask ourselves what the other person is feeling. Becoming good at "reading people" takes time and practice.

DO THIS: Want to know what people feel? Ask them! The question alone already communicates a willingness to empathize, and that's worth a lot. It can be very refreshing and attractive when someone says, "Can I just be really honest with you for a second?" Ask where they're at emotionally, and then genuinely listen to the answer you receive, without judgment.

DON'T DO THIS: Make assumptions. Yes, empathy helps you read body language, but often, no single gesture or expression means anything; if you're talking to a stranger, it's difficult to find patterns in their behavior since you don't have a "baseline" and there's nothing to compare it to. It's easier to just read the room! Pay close attention to how people respond to you in the moment, before you say or do the next thing. This stops you from getting carried away in a monologue or being insensitive to your listener's emotional wavelength. It also gives you time to correct faulty assumptions.

Emotional control

Genuinely charismatic people are never out of control. They always seem to be aware of and in command of themselves, so they never end up losing their temper or indulging in emotional displays they're later embarrassed about. But, this is difficult. How can we be "emotionally expressive" while also controlling our emotions? Don't those contradict?

The truth is that charm and charisma do contain an element of artifice. While charisma may be spontaneous and genuine, it is never unaware. In other words, charismatic people know how to turn the charm on and off, as needed. They know how to "act" to a certain extent, downplaying certain emotions if necessary. For example, they can smile and relax even when they feel nervous, and stay quiet when they know it's no use arguing. Emotional control allows people to stay ultra-calm even in the face of insults or chaos.

DO THIS: Get into the habit of slowing down to breathe. We can blurt things without thinking when we're flustered or overwhelmed, but literally a second or two of deep breathing can center us and remind us that we're in control of how we handle ourselves. Pause before you respond so you can gather yourself.

DON'T DO THIS: Get defensive. Ever. If you're ever feeling in over your head, use humor. Playfully making fun of the situation or dropping in an unexpected quip can defuse tension. Respond to rudeness, mistakes or sudden setbacks (your own or other's!) with lightness. Maintain your emotional "frame" and remind yourself that nothing and nobody can *make* you feel or behave in a certain way. Be less emotionally reactive by just brushing things off instead of getting flustered by them.

Social expressiveness

This refers to sociability and being able to engage and express yourself in social situations. It could mean holding your own in a social group, or public speaking with confidence. Social expressiveness is most often associated with extroversion, but it doesn't need to be – even if you're an introvert, it doesn't mean you can't articulate yourself confidently in social situations. This area may feel challenging for people who don't find socializing easy, but the good news is that it improves with consistent practice.

DO THIS: Yes, it's true that everyone says to "be yourself" and act natural, but for this social skill, it may work to do the opposite: act a little. Watch videos of talk show hosts, standup comedians, actors or public personalities you admire for their charisma. Watch what they do and copy them. Granted, you don't want to base your entire identity on this persona, but it can be a great way to kick start your own innate charisma and give you some practice and confidence.

Consider signing up for a public speaking course, or joining an improv class, dance troupe or amateur drama group. Try standup comedy, an open mic night or simply speak up more in groups. You may be petrified at first, but practice really does make perfect. Frame the exercise as simply having a laugh rather than performing perfectly. You'll lower the stakes and teach yourself not to let fear of failure get in the way.

DON'T DO THIS: Be a slob, i.e., careless with how you dress and present yourself. Much of our communication happens before we even open our mouths. Think about what your clothing and accessories are saying about you, and challenge yourself to take a risk and express your individuality a little more. It may sound too obvious, but many amazing conversations have been spurred by people wearing provocative slogan t-shirts!

Social sensitivity

Just as you can become more masterful in what you communicate to others and how, you can also improve your ability to read what others are broadcasting. An impressive person is nice to *look at* from afar, but a charismatic person is nice to *be with*. When you're in their presence, you feel seen and listened to, you feel that they're the most interesting person you've ever met... and also, somehow, that you are more interesting than you remember!

It's the difference between watching a perfectly choreographed dance performance on a stage, versus being up close and personal with a good dancer, who is dancing *with* us, responding spontaneously and sensitively in every moment. This ability to feel and respond to people dynamically is down to social sensitivity. When people lack this ability, it starts to feel like you're both in separate worlds, having two conversations that have nothing to do with each other.

DO THIS: Practice being sensitive to overall surroundings and context. The next time you're in a new social situation, pause and read the situation before speaking or acting. What is the "energy" of the room? If the group shared one broad emotion and intention at this moment, what would it be? More practically, what are the social conventions and cultural assumptions around this gathering?

Watch people. Devote an hour or so to (unobtrusively) observe others passing by, and just notice what's going on with them. Especially try to read their *emotions*, and how those emotions are reflected in their bodies, faces, voices, everything.

It may sound odd, but meditating can also make you a better listener, which can improve your communication and empathy skills, which can make you more charismatic. Often, we rush into conversations with an agenda or assumptions about who the other person is. However, if you're mindful, you can stop and just look at what is actually in front of you. Drop your expectations, judgments and preconceptions and just neutrally observe what is happening. You may find yourself so much more in tune with others!

DON'T DO THIS: Avoid talking about yourself. Even if you're not bragging or boasting, constantly turning the conversation to *your* ideas, *your* experiences, and *your* opinions is boring. Instead, next time you're tempted to say something about yourself, deliberately choose to ask the other person a question. Most people don't actually conceal themselves; there's a world of fascinating information right there, if you only care to ask!

Social control

Finally, the social role-playing skill that charismatic people are especially good at, which non-charismatic people never even consider: social control. This can be difficult to describe, especially to people who think of social interaction in terms of authenticity and honesty. The truth is, however, that all human social interaction is deliberate, purposeful and rule-bound. In other words, we all play roles – even when we're ourselves!

If you have above-average social control, you're able to skilfully switch roles depending on the situation and your goals. You may play up your artistic, carefree side when on a date, but switch to hard-nosed taskmaster at work, where it matters. You may be very aware of how others perceive you, and choose to gently present a particular version of yourself to them, according to what you're trying to achieve.

Now, for some people, this skill can look dishonest or manipulative – and taken too far, it can be! But you only need to see someone who doesn't possess this skill to understand why it's so important. Do you know "blunt" people who insist on speaking their minds regardless of social context or the negative ramifications? Using a little poise, grace and etiquette is actually an intelligent way to control social situations to your advantage. Don't confuse rudeness, roughness or lack of social awareness with authenticity. At the same time, don't assume that "wearing a mask" is always disingenuous.

DO THIS: Learn to love small talk. Many introverts loathe small talk, and prefer deep, meaty topics. But this is no different from going on a first date and taking your clothes off before you've said hello! Small talk is not small

– it's an important, necessary part of creating trust and rapport with people, so that you can *build* connections over time. To get good at small talk, just practice more. Chat to waiters, people in supermarket lines or the guy on the help line.

DON'T DO THIS: Don't avoid strangers. Challenge yourself to speak to new people as often as you can. Most of us tend to steer clear of interactions with people we don't know, but they can be a rich source of insight and practice for social skills. Don't worry if you encounter awkwardness – charismatic people are unfazed by this and just keep going!

When you encounter a charismatic person, they can initially appear to be outside of the ordinary somehow, as though they are breaking the social rules or doing something very radical. Truthfully, they *are* playing by the rules; they're just playing very well! People can make the mistake of thinking that charisma and magnetism are fixed personal qualities that belong to people, like attractiveness. But really, charisma is *relational* – it's something that emerges in context, in conversations and dynamic interactions with people. That's why we cannot be more charismatic by simply working on ourselves, for example, by dressing nicer. Charisma only happens when we know how to play the social game – and that means it's not about us but about *other people*.

Let's go back to our definition: a charismatic person is one who is **likeable**, and one who can **influence** others. And according to Riggio, they're people who are good at impacting others on an emotional level, because they know how to express themselves, how to perceive others, and how to control the situation. How do you compare to this description?

In the next chapter, we will look at concrete ways to become more charismatic, but before we do, let's take a personal inventory. In a journal or notebook, try to answer the following questions to pinpoint which areas you most need to work on:

To measure your influence

Do I have presence in a room?

Am I able to persuade, convince and influence others?

Am I comfortable with and able to lead a group?

To measure your likeability

Do people generally feel comfortable around me?

Do I smile genuinely and often?

Do I get along with all kinds of people?

To measure emotional skills

Am I emotionally expressive?

Am I able to read, listen to and empathize with the emotions of others?

Am I good at emotional self-regulation, and can I control my feelings (hiding them if necessary?)

To measure social skills

Am I comfortable expressing myself in public, such as in groups?

Am I in tune with social rules, etiquette and cultural contexts?

Do I know how to play a role, wear a mask and control how others perceive me?

If you answer each of the above honestly, you'll start to see a clear picture of where you are currently, and get an idea of what to focus on and improve. Perhaps you discover that you're an emotionally intelligent person with enormous empathy and sensitivity, but you lack confidence in social rules. Maybe you're good at leading and inspiring others, but miss out because you're not likeable – or vice versa!

However you measure up, though, remember that *anyone* can be charismatic, and by understanding your own unique strengths and weaknesses in this area, you've taken a real step towards becoming the most likeable and magnetic version of yourself!

Summary

- Charming people may seem to possess a mysterious quality nobody else does, but charisma is a knowable set of social and emotional behaviors that anyone can learn.
- Charisma can be defined as a blend of likeability and influence. Charismatics have presence in a room, can impact and persuade others, can lead, but also know how to put people at ease, are warm, smile often, and get along with anyone.
- Practice taking up more space in a room, and examine any core beliefs that may negatively impact your posture and expression. Believe deep down that other people are not a threat and that you have something worthwhile to communicate.
- Speak openly about your passions, and when you address others, speak to their highest selves. Smile often and remember the details of what people tell you.
- Don't interrupt, judge, complain, gossip or express negativity. Instead, express gratitude and optimism.
- Ronald Riggio broke charisma into 3 social and emotional functions: expressiveness, sensitivity to other people's expressiveness, and self-control.
- To be more charismatic, express yourself emotionally with colorful language and dynamic facial expressions. Pay attention to people's nonverbal expression, but don't

be afraid to ask directly about how others feel.

- To improve emotional control, slow down, breathe and become present, rather than reacting mindlessly.
- Acting and improv can help you improve social skills, and the ability to consciously wear a social mask. Pay attention to how you're physically presenting yourself and dress with care and deliberation.
- Finally, learn to "people watch" and get into the habit of asking more questions instead of talking about yourself in conversations.

Chapter 2: Building real-world charisma

We've fleshed out a usable definition of charisma and broken it down into its parts. And hopefully, you've been able to zoom in on all those parts of charisma that you're already getting right... and those that need a little more work. This leads us to the obvious next question: how do we get better?

First things first: your charisma won't look like anyone else's charisma. This makes sense – think of any famous charismatic people from history, and they're all different from one another; Marilyn Monroe, Stalin and Steve Jobs were all enigmatic characters, but in very different ways! This is precisely what Olivia Fox Cabane, author of *The Charisma Myth*, found, i.e., that there are different types of charisma. She listed four general categories, but even within these groups, it's easy to see the endless possible variations:

The focused charismatic

This is someone who places deep, undivided attention on others, and makes them feel like "the most important person in the room." Talk show hosts build their brands on this kind of charisma, as do motivational speakers – and cult leaders! You'll know this is your preferred charisma style if you're often told you're a good listener. Focus charismatics are people that know that the best way to shine is to show off others to their best. If you often find yourself in the guru role of guiding people to be the best they can be, this may be your strong area.

The visionary charismatic

Recall Riggio's theory about emotional and social expressiveness – we are drawn to those who can move us to see their inspiring vision of the future, especially if they have the enthusiasm and energy to campaign for that vision. Think about Steve Jobs building a following devoted to his vision of the future, or Martin Luther King Junior's rousing speeches. Innovators and creative people can excel at visionary charisma, too, since they need to convince others to buy into a vision that only they can see. If you've ever managed to get people rallied together on a passion project, and if your visions seem infectious, you might have this type of charisma.

The kind charismatic

Emotional connection is powerful stuff – think of the Dalai Lama and how profoundly he influences people without conventional trappings of wealth and power. He does so purely on an emotional level, with genuine warmth and compassion. If you're a person who can drastically elevate situations with kindness, mercy, empathy and benevolence, this form of charisma may be your strongest.

The authoritative charismatic

Finally, a more classic picture of a charismatic leader – like Stalin or Hitler, people with this style of influence use power and status to position themselves as authorities, experts or leaders. Such people seem to naturally command control, and effortlessly lead others. Do you frequently find that other people defer to your judgment or put you in charge of important tasks? You might be better at exuding this kind of charisma than the other types.

Now, this isn't to say that these are the only types. If you think of famous charismatics from history, you'll find many that don't fit the mold. Some may inspire and lead people because of their bravery and strength (sporting heroes; those who beat the odds after disease or injury), some may captivate and enthrall people with immense beauty, grace or sex appeal (the starlets from Hollywood's Golden Era), others may capture people's admiration through humor, creativity or originality (Robin Williams' comic genius could hit on an emotional level) and others may garner attention because they're moral or even spiritual crusaders (think of how Greta Thunberg commanded a room with her righteous indignation about climate change).

What about you? You may not yet feel confident in your own charismatic abilities, but you're probably beginning to get a sense for the *style* of that potential charisma, according to your own personality, values and experiences. The lesson here is that you shouldn't worry too much if you don't quite see yourself in the conventional descriptions of "charismatic leader" – you can be an engaging, fascinating person with a massive presence in a room, in a way that's all your own!

Fox Cabane's approach

Olivia Fox Cabane's model of charisma is pretty simple. She suggests that there are just three main components:

POWER

PRESENCE

WARMTH

Power is here defined as the capacity to impact others, while presence is the ability to be fully engaged and attentive to the moment. Finally, warmth is about perceived goodwill or benevolence, or the degree to which people believe you will use your power and presence in their best interest. Again, all three of these are primarily emotional and about how people *feel* – charisma is not rational!

We can recognize these factors as analogous to the influence, presence and affability we discussed in the last chapter. From Cabane's point of view, different charisma styles vary in their relative proportions of these three special ingredients. For example, authoritative charismatics tend to blow everyone out of the water when it comes to power and presence, but tend to be a little weaker on warmth. Kind and focused charismatics excel in emotional warmth but may lack a little in the power department.

Once you have an idea of your current charisma quotient, and a few clues on your personal style, you have two options for improving yourself:

1. You can lean into your unique style and amplify it
2. You can balance out by cultivating those aspects you lack, so you're more rounded

Either way, always keep in mind that charisma is most powerful when it's personal and genuine, so keep checking in with your authentic values, the things that fire you up, and your natural gifts. With that in mind, let's look at some practical exercises to start tapping into your inner charm. Use these the next time you're heading into a meeting, going on a date, spending time with friends or family or speaking in public.

Exercise 1: Make yourself comfortable

We've seen that charismatic people are confident and have presence. They trust in themselves and their message, and they unapologetically take up space in the room. On a very basic level, though, confidence = comfort. It means being at home in your own skin, at ease with others, and comfortable in the world in general. This is why people advise to "walk into a room like you own it." Because when you are comfortable, you can *relax and expand* your awareness outwards to engage emotionally with others. When you're uncomfortable, every fiber of your being will communicate that, and act as a barrier to your power, presence and warmth.

Start simple and think about what you're wearing. It's infinitely better to wear something you're genuinely comfy in rather than a nice outfit that's too scratchy, too tight, too restrictive or too awkward. For Cabane, physical and mental discomfort are the biggest obstacles to building charisma. And physical tension *will* manifest as social and emotional tension. Think also about your general physical wellbeing. Ensure that you're not hungry or thirsty, tired, ill or too hot/cold. If you're going to be outside, plan ahead to make sure you're not distracted by the sun glaring in your eyes, or the wind blowing your hair around, or the wrong footwear.

Before you head out to a social interaction, pause for a moment and check in with yourself, body and mind. Remind yourself that how things *look* is not as important as how they *feel*. A silk tie or a gorgeous evening gown might be conventional symbols of style and good taste, but if they make you feel bad, then that is what you will transmit socially. Make sure that your physical situation supports you and allows you to express yourself freely, with minimal distraction. If something is getting in the way, get rid of it.

Exercise 2: Use ritual and visualization

Being charismatic is a state of mind. And just like an athlete needs to warm up before a big game or race, you need to warm up emotionally and psychologically before you wow everyone with charm. To extend the metaphor, if you jump into a marathon without stretching beforehand, you're going to be creaky and potentially injure yourself. Likewise, if you just jump into a challenging social situation without any thought or planning, you're going to fumble.

Ritual can be the perfect "social warm up." Not only does it allow us to get into the right mindset, but the mere fact of us planning ahead, taking charge and paying deliberate attention to our strategy will make us feel more in control and more confident. Remember that charisma is a social game, and the best players are those that take it seriously!

What kind of ritual is best? That depends on the state of mind you're trying to cultivate.

Imagine an important job interview coming up and wanting to dazzle your interviewers. It's a sales position, so you need to display both authoritative and focused charisma to charm the interviews and show them you know how to do the job. Truthfully, you're feeling nervous and unsure of yourself, so you know that you're going to need to demonstrate immense social and emotional control.

Hours before the interview, you start psyching yourself up. You listen to energizing music you know always puts you in a good mood. You run over a few mantras and affirmations to focus your mind. You plan your outfit and practice a few responses in a mirror. Finally, you spend time in active visualization. This could go a few different ways: you might imagine in detail how you want the interview to go, seeing yourself smiling, confidently taking charge of the room, and mentally rehearsing your posture, tone of voice and overall attitude.

You could also visualize someone you admire and who demonstrates the mindset you're trying to convey. You could picture being that person, as though you're temporarily using their persona as a mask to give you confidence. What would that person say and do in this situation? You could also use more abstract visualization, for example, imagining in vivid detail that all the stress is leaving your body in the form of literal negative words that float away off the surface of your skin, while a warm glow comes up from the ground and fills you up with energy, conviction and confidence. After the visualization, you imagine that this warmth stays with you, and that you carry it into the interview like a powerful talisman or magic spell. Speaking of talismans, maybe you have a lucky charm or special ritual that helps make the occasion feel auspicious – you wear a sentimental accessory, treat yourself, light a candle, say a prayer or plan to do something rewarding afterwards.

Exercise 3: Be present, build presence

Fox Cabane has a slightly different take on the idea of presence. For her, a person builds presence when they themselves are... present. This means being fully anchored in the moment, rather than having your attention elsewhere. The more present you are, the more genuinely you can engage others, respond sensitively to minute changes in the conversational flow, and observe others' emotional states. It's also far easier to be felt as warm if you are present, focused and paying attention to the person in front of you!

If you guessed that mindfulness practice will help with presence, then you guessed right. Anxiety can kill your charismatic aura because it takes you out of the moment – and the moment is exactly where the people you need to connect with are! Mindfulness is a tool that can help you reduce anxiety and boost awareness whether you practice it alone, in preparation for a social situation, or in that situation as it unfolds.

Again, the way you use mindfulness depends on your aims. Consider the following examples.

A person trying to improve their warmth and affability realizes that judgment gets in the way of them connecting with people. They try a "loving kindness" meditation every morning, where they practice extending compassion and understanding to everyone. Sitting quietly and with focus, they imagine a person they love, and focus on this feeling of acceptance and warmth. Then, they imagine someone they only like, but practice feeling this same warmth for them, too. Next, they imagine someone they are neutral about, and so on, until they reach a person they actively dislike. They work hard to find feelings of kindness for them, and for the fact that they are human beings who deserve compassion and respect regardless.

While such a person may find that this practice generally improves their outlook and makes them more tolerant and accepting people, another might simply commit to finding little "windows" of awareness in every social interaction. Pausing, coming to the present and reminding themselves to be aware of their body and breath in the moment, they become more relaxed and dynamically engaged. Perhaps they notice that their voice or body language is conveying stress, so they consciously choose to loosen up. Perhaps they realize they're hogging the conversation and graciously decide to let the other person take the stage for a while.

One great way of building presence is to *take your time.* Anxiety, lack of presence, and rushing all go hand in hand. If you find yourself feeling tense in a moment, just pause. Breathe. Anchor in the present and in your 5 senses. What can you smell? See? Taste, even? Slow down and just get comfy in the moment. It's usually our stressful ruminations about how we are in social situations that derail us, and not the situation itself. Anchor in the moment and let these ruminations drift away. Finally, put your attention squarely on the other person – don't let your mind wander, and don't get distracted by your phone.

Exercise 4: Take care

This is an extension of the previous exercise. When you pause, you give yourself the chance to act deliberately rather than reactively. You stop being at the mercy of knee-jerk reactions and start to act consciously – congratulations, this is the beginning of that elusive quality called grace and poise! For example, if somebody says something that catches you off guard and embarrasses you a little, don't immediately blush and blurt out something that makes you sound defensive. Rather, pause and think, "how do I want to play this?" and then choose to laugh it off, deflect attention by saying something amusing or graciously thank the person for their comment, completely changing the energy of the interaction. But you can only do all this if you're aware enough to pause in the first place.

Every choice you make in a social interaction matters. Your body language, your tone of voice, your word choice, your facial expression. Rather than being intimidated by this fact, use it to your advantage – see all of these as colors on a palette to paint the image *you* want to paint. Don't leave anything to chance. Take care with how you dress, how you speak, and how you're holding yourself in conversations. Especially take care of what is happening with people around you and your effect on them. Again, we're in the realm of social control, which cannot be achieved without a degree of mindful awareness.

Pause before you respond – just a few seconds, and you'll seem more poised and put together. Instead of saying "um" simply keep quiet while thinking of what to say. If you are confident enough to take your time speaking, people will usually respond in kind and pay more attention to your words. Finally, be careful about your word choice, and consider your audience. It's always a good idea to match your tone, word choice, volume and pitch to theirs if you're unsure.

Howard Friedman's approach

University of California professor of psychology Howard Friedman has spent decades researching various social behaviors, particularly this elusive quality we call charisma. He developed the Affective Communication Test (appropriately called ACT), which he believed was a good indicator of people's emotional expressiveness, i.e., their overall charisma. Like Riggio, Friedman believed that there is something compelling and attractive about people who easily and comfortably **express** themselves. In a 1980 paper published in the *Journal of Personality and Social Psychology*, he and Riggio, together with two fellow researchers, found that nonverbal expressiveness plays a big role in social interactions.

Whichever form it takes, communicating with spiritedness, energy, passion, eloquence and vibrant gestures all make a person far more charismatic. Remembering that charisma is about impacting others emotionally, it's easy to see why expressiveness is so important – it allows us to more easily affect others, leading and captivating and inspiring them. Words matter, but when they're paired with *nonverbal* expression, they can be charismatic. It's as though charming people are fluent in two languages: the obvious superficial one and the more primal, unspoken and nonverbal one that captivates us more easily.

The ACT is pretty simple: there are ten statements that participants are asked to respond to, noting the extent to which they agree. You can try it yourself by seeing the degree to which the following statements apply to you (note that these are inspired by several different versions of the test):

When I hear good music, I can't help but move my body

When I laugh, it's jovial and buoyant, and everyone can hear me

When I'm on the phone, my mood and feelings come across loud and clear

In conversations with friends, I am tactile and easily touch or hug people

I don't mind when a group of people notice me or watch me

I usually have an obvious facial expression, and am seldom neutral

People often tell me I'd make a good actor or actress

I'm not shy and don't mind being the center of attention

I know how to look at people seductively if I want to

I've always been good at playing games like charades or miming

Strangers often think I'm younger than I am

The more strongly you agree to the above statements, the more likely you're perceived as charismatic. These statements essentially measure your nonverbal affective expressiveness. Let's look more closely at what this expressiveness actually looks like in the real world, and how you can go about cultivating some of it in yourself.

Kinesthetic responsiveness

People are drawn to and enthralled by displays of health, vigor, and liveliness in a very primal sense. Think of how people can't tear their eyes away from a talented performer, a passionate dancer or singer, or someone throwing their heart and soul into something special. We're attracted to people that seem to be filled to the brim with passion and energy – perhaps we hope that some of it will rub off on us!

Before human beings invented language, they communicated with their bodies. In fact, you could say that movement is a more primitive and immediate form of communication. Kinesthetic responsiveness is about expressing yourself emotionally through your body's movement. Boring and unengaging people seem to be dead from the neck down. They slump and appear stagnant – their bodies don't seem to extend or expand much into the space around them. In contrast, charismatic people are *embodied*, and their enthusiasm manifests in *all* of them. They move. They gesture. They shift in their seats, tilt their heads, or flap their hands around madly when telling an amusing story.

DO THIS: Stay in shape. No really! If you're healthy and physically active, you'll be more confident and at ease in your own skin, lighter on your feet and more mobile. As you speak to anyone, remember that your body is also constantly sending a message. Do you want that message to be, "zzzz, I'm half asleep..."?

Expressive and contagious laugh

A laugh is a powerful thing. It can make people fall in love, put them at ease, make them trust you... it can make *them* laugh. Why is a genuine, juicy laugh so infectious? Well, think about what a laugh is: a simple, direct expression of joy. It shows a person that, just for one unguarded moment, is genuinely expressing how they feel. Also, it's a potent communication that you're happy, resilient, healthy and able to enjoy yourself. People who are miserable, anxious or in the habit of denying themselves pleasure are not attractive, and they're not charismatic. But when you hear a person laugh from their core, something happens to you – you want to be a part of it! You're drawn in closer. All barriers and conventions temporarily fall away, and a moment of intimacy is possible.

DO THIS: Commit to never stifling a laugh. Be free and ebullient with your joy and let it overflow when you feel it, without a second thought for how you look or for social appropriateness (within reason, of course... bursting out laughing at a funeral is probably not a good idea). You could even practice by watching funny videos or comedy, and letting yourself laugh openly. The next time you're in company and want to laugh, don't force or fake anything: genuine and spontaneous joy is like charisma gold dust – don't hide it!

Expressive voice

Have you noticed how pets and other animals don't care about the words you say to them, but seem to respond only to the tone and pitch of your voice? Human animals are no different! Whether we're conscious of it or not, we all respond to the emotion we hear in other people's voices, regardless of the words they're using. If your words are saying one thing and your voice is communicating another, people will perceive the mismatch, and it will put them on edge; they may interpret the discrepancy as insincerity. This is why it's important to communicate with your whole body – and your voice is an especially important part of your body.

DO THIS: Never speak carelessly. Instead, think about the emotion you're trying to convey and make sure your voice expresses that. Through your tone of voice alone, let people know that you're excited to talk to them, that your conversation brings you pleasure, and that you're fascinated by what they're saying. An old trick for when you're on the phone: even though people can't see you, smile anyway. They will be able to hear it in your voice.

Expressive touching

When we communicate, we are reaching from our world out into the void to touch someone else's world. And the most obvious and concrete way to do this is to... literally touch them. Clearly, this comes with some caveats. Touch needs to be appropriate to work – lightly brushing someone's hand, upper arms or shoulder in the course of events can bridge distances, so to speak, and make the interaction feel more real and present. If touch is pushy or awkward, though, it can prove disastrous.

DO THIS: With people you don't know very well, communicate warmth and presence by touching them just once or twice in a conversation, on the shoulders, hands or lower arms. Naturally weave the touch into another expressive gesture, for example, a light touch when you are indicating "you" or a gentle nudge on the shoulder as you walk through a door to suggest they go first. The trick is to be casual and comfortable in yourself as you do so. If you can't touch without being stiff or uncomfortable, avoid it for a while.

DON'T DO THIS: A caveat here – touch will be received differently depending on whether a man or woman is toucher or touchee. As a rule, like it or not, men can get away with far less touch than women can, and it's usually better to touch someone of the same sex to avoid misunderstanding.

Relax into being in the limelight

If you're shy or an introvert, having all eyes turned on can feel pretty scary. But charismatic people soak up attention easily and with pleasure. Being put on the spot can be nerve-wracking, but even if you're not a natural performer, you can fake it somewhat. Protesting, being awkward or shyly trying to wriggle out of attention actually make things worse. A lot worse! So just relax. Something to remember is that when people turn their attention to you, their intentions are usually benign. Watch a nervous newbie comedian on stage for the first time. Usually, the crowd is generous with their laughs anyway – they *want* the performer to succeed and feel comfortable.

DO THIS: Use humor. You don't have to suddenly think of something witty to say on the spot. Just smile, relax, and breathe. Whatever you do, don't make a big deal of any awkwardness in the moment, or you'll amplify it. Maybe playfully make fun of yourself or the situation. If everyone has turned to look at you after a slip and fall, just get up, smile, take a bow and say, "ta da!" It's not original, it's not even all that funny, but it puts people at ease and will make them smile.

Communicate with your face

While you might find an inscrutable and mysterious person interesting for a little while, you'll soon get bored of how little they're revealing of themselves. Communication is about being engaged – people want to know that they're affecting you, that you have an opinion, and that you are alive and responsive. Think about being on a date; it's excruciating to be with an unreadable person, and not know how they feel about you. It's far more attractive to be with someone who is letting you know loud and clear where they are emotionally.

DO THIS: Speak less, and emote more. It could be as simple as smiling and nodding instead of saying "yes" or lifting a single eyebrow when someone asks your opinion of a movie. Expressing emotions via the face becomes easier the more you practice – look in the mirror and try to see how many different kinds of smiles you can make. Or, the next time you're in a conversation, replace "uh huh" sounds with expressions that mirror or respond to the speaker's.

Change your attitude to strangers

Public speaking coach Sims Wyeth did a survey and found that those who called themselves introverts actually prefer the company of extroverts. Trouble is, extroverts also prefer the company of extroverts! This suggests that it's simply easier and more fun to be with someone socially outgoing and expressive. While there's nothing wrong with being an introvert, the truth is that it can put further distance between you and others, and limit the closeness, engagement and presence required for charisma.

DO THIS: Make the first move. Say hello to strangers first. This may seem scary, but it actually puts you in the driver's seat and gives you more control over social interactions. Practice broaching the silence with new people, and you'll see that the *earlier* you break the ice, the easier the interaction tends to be.

Flirt a little

Friedman believed that charismatic people are experts at using a "seductive glance." While hard to describe, we all know this look when we see it! Sure, there is a strong link between being charismatic and being sexy, alluring or attractive to the opposite sex. But charismatic people are also masters at what could be called "platonic flirting." They flirt with everyone—if we broaden our definition of "flirt."

DO THIS: Practice platonic flirting – with family, friends, children, old people and people you don't even like. Think back to how much razer focus, warmth and sparkle you've brought to romantic dates in the past, and then bring that dazzling (non-sexual) version of yourself into the everyday. Be generous and sincere in the compliments you give. Smile at people often and praise them. Laugh at their jokes. Basically, demonstrate that just being around them *gives you pleasure*. This makes people feel like a million bucks, and like they're seen and appreciated. This kind of non-romantic "chemistry" is wonderful to see in action!

Ham it up

Finally, Friedman identified one form of emotional expressiveness that is the more fundamental precursor to body language: pantomime. Physically acting out a narrative is a brilliant and simple way to add color, life and dynamism to your stories, and to make you seem more relatable, more amusing and way more captivating. You can learn to do this by watching the pros: improv artists, comedians, clowns, impersonators and… two-year-olds, who are the reigning champions of the acting world.

DO THIS: The next time you're relating a story to someone, gradually try to incorporate gestures, actions, voices and movements to add dimension. This can be subtle; for example, if you're relating a discussion between two people, slightly move your position in space and change your voice and posture when you act out each person's part. Make liberal use of dramatic pauses, facial expressions and gestures. It may seem silly, but imagine you're telling the story to a group of excited toddlers and *exaggerate*.

Howard Friedman's approach to charisma homes in on the emotional expressiveness aspect of charisma, and judging by his research, this may be the most significant factor when it comes to charming and engaging people.

It's easy to imagine an emotionally expressive car salesman, stand-up comedian, preacher, politician or celebrity with a megawatt smile. But you may be starting to wonder: is there no room for those people who are quieter, calmer, more sophisticated, more refined, shy, reserved... or plain old timid?

A word on introversion
First, the bad news: charisma is about emotionally impacting others, and it's almost impossible to do that if you're not literally reaching out to others, taking the risk of showing yourself, and being interested in the people around you. Very few can manage to be

aloof and dismissive of others and yet liked. So, if you consider yourself a naturally reclusive or introverted person, then there's no question: you will have to come out of your comfort zone and play a role that may not feel comfortable at first – if you want to increase your charisma, that is.

But the good news? Extroverts have to do this work too. Many shy people falsely assume that extroverts find all this easy. A few do, but if you ask most social butterflies, they'll tell you that they had to work on it. Sometimes constantly! Even the most confident and enigmatic person can sometimes feel vulnerable, crabby, unconfident, or socially terrified. The difference is they understand there's no way around it: like anything in life, it takes consistent practice, humility and the willingness to learn.

There's more good news, though. You *don't* have to be an overbearing or fake loudmouth to be charismatic. You can keep your quiet, calm personality and still be alluring. "Extroverts sparkle, introverts glow." Being naturally less gregarious is no excuse for not mastering warmth, sensitivity, good communication, listening skills, tact and expressiveness. In fact, there are a few aspects of charisma that you may be *better* equipped to master than your extroverted brethren! In our next chapter, we'll look at two case studies that prove that charm comes in many flavors, and introversion/extroversion has very little to do with it.

Summary

- Olivia Fox Cabane explains how there are four charisma types according to the proportion of power, presence and warmth. The focused charismatic (who pays deep attention to others), the visionary charismatic (who communicates their infectious passion), the kind charismatic (who inspires with warmth and compassion) and the authoritative charismatic (who leads others with expertise and power).
- Depending on your goals, you can play up your natural charisma strengths or seek to balance out your weaknesses.
- To be socially and emotionally comfortable, plan ahead and make sure you're physically comfortable, which will remove barriers to charismatic connection.
- Use ritual and visualization as a "social warm up." Music, meditation, and affirmations can help you prepare.

- Build presence with mindfulness. Slow down, breathe and anchor in the senses. Pause before you respond, and take conscious care of every detail of the interaction, including your verbal and nonverbal expression, appearance, and behavior.
- Howard Friedman emphasized the affective, nonverbal expressiveness component of charisma.
- Communicate with *all* your body and laugh openly. Speak with a dynamic, varied voice that changes in pitch, tone and expression. Use touch to bridge distance and create warmth, aware that the rules differ for men and women.
- Speak less and emote more via facial expression. If you find yourself the center of attention, relax and don't draw attention to awkwardness, using humor to defuse tension. Use exaggerated, pantomime-like gestures and initiate contact with strangers. Finally, practice the art of "platonic flirting."
- Introverts *can* be charismatic, but they must do so on their own terms.

Chapter 3: Putting it all together

In chapters 1 and 2, we looked at several different models and theories that could help us better grasp the charisma phenomenon. We considered the researchers at the University of Toronto and their *General Charisma Inventory* outlining affability and influence aspects. We examined Riggio's model, which put expressiveness, sensitivity and control as the three tasks of charisma, whether applied to emotional aspects or social ones. We explored Olivia Fox Cabane's Power-Presence-Warmth trinity and looked at some of her practical exercises for visualization and ritual. Finally, we looked at Friedman's theory, which focused on "affective communication," and how charismatic people are those that express themselves nonverbally.

Well, that's a lot to take in! How can we pull all this together into something that will make a difference in our lives? Each of these theories is a blend of explanation, description of traits, and suggestions for practical exercises we can all try to become more charismatic. In this chapter, we synthesize the best of each theory and create our own meta-theory. Below we'll look at the *five traits most consistently associated with charisma.* Consider it a cheat sheet:

Trait 1: Likeability and warmth

Or "affability." Arguably the most important trait. If you can smile, put people at ease and accept others for who they are, you're already halfway there.

Challenge yourself to smile at a stranger every day. Look for ways to laugh and be light-hearted. Commit right now to never being that person who gossips, criticizes or judges people in public. Instead, make it a habit to genuinely learn what others can teach you in every interaction, and take it upon yourself to shine the light of your attention on others, so they feel seen, appreciated, and listened to.

Trait 2: Power and influence

The ability to convince and persuade others, and being perceived as competent and in control. The only chance you have of being an inspirational presence in people's lives, and to have them believe in you, is to start with belief in *yourself*. Tap into those things you know with all your heart, the skills you're a natural expert at, and the values that mean more than anything to you. Find your raw, sparkling passion and communicate it loud and clear to others – think of influence as the transmission of conviction from one person to another. But you must have that conviction in the first place!

Trait 3: Emotional intelligence

Charisma is not about logic, intelligence, or being right. It's about emotions. Being emotionally intelligent means knowing how to perceive the emotions of others, as well as ensuring that your own are communicated. Charismatic people don't just rely on words – they can engage emotionally on nonverbal channels.

The single best way to ramp up your emotional intelligence is to get into your body. Use all of yourself to communicate, including your voice, posture, movement, and gesture. Likewise, watch closely how other people present themselves – all of themselves. Listening is about close conscious awareness, and the perception of patterns that go beyond the words people say.

Trait 4: Presence, awareness and self-control

Anxiety, distraction, assumption, expectation and getting stuck in our own heads... all of this take us out of the moment, and saps our charisma. Charm is something living and dynamic that unfolds in the moment; if we hope to master it, we need to be spontaneous, alive to the moment and responsive. This takes a degree of self-awareness. We can improve our ability to anchor in the moment and the person in front of us by using mindfulness techniques. Once we're routinely aware of ourselves, we can do the next thing: control ourselves.

Awareness paves the way for us to consciously choose how we want to appear, speak, and engage. What role do we want to play and why? What mask shall we wear, and what are the rules of the game we're playing?

Trait 5: Social intelligence and leadership

When we master ourselves in any social interaction, we earn the right to begin to steer things in the direction we want them to go. In other words, we become capable of leadership. In a way, the ability to lead is a culmination of all the charismatic traits, and is the intelligent synthesizing of all the social and emotional skills into one. If we have a vision, we can reach out to others, communicate it, and persuade them to help us build that vision.

Most of us want to be more charismatic because we just want people to like us. But charisma can also be applied – when we put energy, brilliance and warmth to work, what could we achieve and create? It's powerful stuff!

A prince and a queen – two case studies

In West Philadelphia, born and raised, this particular celebrity spent most of his days charming the pants off people. First busting onto the TV screen as the *Fresh Prince of Bel Air*, Will Smith has since won four Grammy Awards and been nominated for countless others. Will Smith is arguably one of the most recognizable and likeable actors (and rappers!) globally and has built his $250 million empire on one thing: his personality.

Will Smith is one charismatic guy. Picture him in your head right now – what do you see? Most likely, you envision a broad, easy smile. Smith is the quintessential "larger than life" personality and someone who can teach us a lot about thriving at the center of attention. How does Will measure up against our 5 ultra-charisma traits?

Likeability? Check. Emotional intelligence and presence? Check and check. In fact, Smith admirably demonstrates all these characteristics. His power and influence seem to come from his unapologetically being himself – and making it look so good that other people are inspired to imitate him!

Although the comedic actor gives off an easy-going aura, his success was *not* accidental. According to him, you need to be prepared. Take charge and decide how you want life to play out *before* it happens. "So if you stay ready, you ain't gotta get ready, and that is how I run my life. Just stay ready. Stay in shape and then you don't have to rush to train before the movie starts ...And I'll show you my abs later because I'm in shape. But that idea, if you stay ready, you don't have to get ready." Will Smith is paying attention, he's being present, and he's committed to learning the rules of the game so that when it's time to play, he's ready to go. He's in control. Sure, he may play it cool and joke around, but deep down, there is a hard-nosed willingness to visualize what he wants, and to do the work required. "In my mind, I've always been an A-list Hollywood superstar. Y'all just didn't know yet."

Will Smith uses lashings of humor to keep things light and humble – and though it doesn't look like a fine art, it really is. "My daughter said, 'Daddy, are we rich?' I say, 'No, baby, you're broke. Daddy worked really hard. You don't even own them clothes. Mommy and daddy are going to teach you how to create a space where you have the life that you desire, but this is the life that mommy and daddy desired, and we worked really hard to create this life for ourselves, but you are going to have to create your own.'" See how he speaks to his passion and conviction, but never gets too serious or allows it to come across as arrogance? This is the power of well-placed humor.

Will Smith is off the charts when it comes to likeability. He's the kind of mega-celebrity you could imagine being friends with, and is frequently reported as being approachable and friendly to those who want autographs or pictures. Watch any recorded interviews with him, and you'll see that he takes the same relaxed, respectful and easy approach with everyone, no matter who they are. He looks them in the eyes, talks plainly and without airs, and keeps smiling. Because he is so at ease with himself, others feel relaxed around him. A little humor, open body language, a warm smile, and the occasional moment of deep sincerity all make for a pretty charming package. It's what makes Will Smith feel like something even better than a famous celebrity – that is, a genuinely awesome person.

So, where does this leave us? If you want to have superstar A-list energy and impressive charisma, do you have to start acting like Will Smith? *Absolutely not.*

Consider this: who else is like Will Smith? You may be able to think of a few people a bit like him (Eddie Murphy comes to mind), but Will Smith's personal brand is all his own. He took the way he looked, his personality, his accent, everything, and *owned* it. Can you imagine Will Smith before he was famous, trying to fake his way into celebrity by mimicking someone like Humphrey Bogart? Just picture it: Will Smith, speaking kind of like Frank Sinatra, wearing a suit and tie, and crooning in front of a big brass band. It doesn't even make sense, right?

Or picture Will Smith trying to be a dangerous "bad boy" and playing up his sex appeal like countless other celebrities he could have taken inspiration from. It just doesn't work. Instead, Will Smith took who he was and ran with it. His brand is "clean" and fun, and nobody does Will Smith better than he does! In a way, Smith made an exaggerated mask of his own personality, and played that role to perfection. He achieved levels of likeability and fame that he never would have if he merely imitated someone else.

If this inspires you, the lesson is to find your unique brand of charm, and play it up to the max. Being "larger than life" in *your* life may look nothing like it does for Will Smith, but it's still built on the same 5 charisma traits that he mastered.

So, that's our "prince" covered – who is our "queen"?

While Will Smith grabs the limelight with his bold, confident and in-your-face charisma, our next celebrity is a study in charisma that is more magnetic – i.e., it doesn't expand out into the world so much as invite other people to *come closer*.

Jane Fonda told the New York Times about the aura around Marilyn Monroe, who she had met in an acting class. Apparently, people at a party who were once waiting for Monroe to arrive were so excited that some were physically shaking. The actress purportedly told people she could switch her charm off and on, disappearing invisibly into a subway and not being noticed one moment, and behaving in such a way the next moment that people were falling over themselves to get a look at her.

Today, countless celebrities have been influenced by the original sex symbol, and one could argue her legacy is overplayed at this point. It's easy to forget, however, just how impressive Monroe's achievements were at the time – she literally transformed herself into a goddess of the screen, the likes of which nobody had ever seen before. If charisma was a skill, Marilyn Monroe was one of its first heavyweight geniuses.

Like Will Smith, her dazzling aura came down to the irresistible persona she portrayed. But that's where the similarities end. Whereas Smith is loud, confident and funny, Monroe was far more low-key. In interviews, she was gentle, soft-spoken, a little mysterious and flirtatious... even, bizarrely, conveying a fragile and vulnerable sense of innocence that somehow just seemed to make her more gorgeous. Monroe grew up poor, brunette and with crushingly low self-esteem that remained with her even after her mega-stardom. She suffered horribly from stage-fright and probably would not have considered herself an extrovert in the least.

And yet! Monroe didn't need to search for attention because it always seemed to find her. She was magnetic – she simply was her dazzling self, and people couldn't help but be drawn towards her. A reporter once said, "Amid a slowly gathering hush, she stood there, a blond apparition in a strapless cocktail gown, a little breathless as if she were

Cinderella, just stepped from the pumpkin coach." No funny quips, no performance. She didn't *do* anything in particular. She just was.

So, what can we learn from Marilyn (especially those of us who want to create a quieter, more alluring magnetism)? Well, it probably doesn't hurt to be astoundingly beautiful. But other beautiful actresses surrounded Marilyn, and she still outshone them. Elizabeth Taylor, Audrey Hepburn and Sophia Loren were certainly formidable competition, but none had that ineffable star quality that Marilyn did. Why?

Marilyn was an actress, but her best role was off-screen, where she successfully created a dazzling sex-siren image. Like Will Smith, none of this was by accident. Marilyn Monroe wasn't born Marilyn Monroe. She spent enormous amounts of energy and time crafting her image; watch any of her gestures, idiosyncrasies and manners of speech in interviews – every inch of it is carefully considered, rehearsed and delivered with precision.

And she did it *without* being loud or larger than life. She was the queen of the seductive glance, the irresistible laugh, and dressing in such a way that you couldn't help but notice her. She used her sex appeal, yes, but it's interesting to note that Marilyn's biggest fans today are seemingly women, who are just as entranced by her vision of femininity, proving that raw sex appeal was only part of her charm.

If you can't see yourself cultivating an "out there" brand of charm like Will Smith, consider a more magnetic, passive charismatic such as Marilyn as your inspiration. Get people to come to you. One way to do this is to use your appearance – how can you immediately set yourself apart from other people without speaking a word? Ramp up your presence in a room by being *visually unusual*, in whatever way fits your personality best. It takes a little courage to be different, but many introverted or shy people find it easier to "express" themselves this way, since it doesn't require them to be brash and talkative. It may seem superficial to focus a lot on your appearance, but this is one of the most immediate and primal ways we communicate nonverbally.

Another thing we can learn from Marilyn is the power of crafting an image. The icon she created had very little to do with who she actually was as a person – reportedly a very intelligent, complex humanitarian. Marilyn played a role. Today, celebrities like Beyonce have admitted to doing the same thing, for example, when they get on stage, they are no longer themselves, but an alter ego. This is something that allows even painfully shy people to be terrific actors – when it's not *you* that you're putting out there, it's so much easier to take risks! You can do the same by creating your own alter-ego. Make this other person a kind of archetype, or a glamorous, brilliant version of yourself. Ask what they would do in a social interaction, then do it.

There's one final part of Marilyn Monroe's charm that it would be a mistake to leave out, which is her story's tragic element. Everyone knows that Marilyn was troubled, misunderstood, and haunted by her past— behind the glitz and glamor. There were suggestions of drug use, and her love life was tumultuous. She died young and in tragic and mysterious circumstances, and today people think wistfully about her legacy – who was the *real* Marilyn?

This is all to say that being charismatic doesn't necessarily mean that you are perfect, happy and uncomplicated. The fact that Marilyn's charming façade and her real self were at such odds doesn't detract from her appeal – it adds to it! In other words, we all find a little drama, mystery and darkness extremely enticing. She portrayed a beautiful, flawless image, but she is today loved for the fact that much of her life *wasn't* beautiful and flawless. People love Marilyn because she was vulnerable, imperfect and tragic. We feel touched that she suffered, not that her life was easy.

If you feel like you are too boring, flawed, insecure, or unhappy to be a truly charismatic person, think again. If you can consciously and deliberately show your vulnerability to others, you can come across as infinitely more human, more likeable and more real than if you had stayed completely cool and invincible. Especially for women, a degree of fragility can be extremely becoming. It's OK to be a little self-deprecating, or to humorously own up to your fears and weaknesses. Don't be afraid to show your soft side now and then. Done right, this can be incredibly charming!

Designing your unique charisma formula

Now, what about you?

You have your own, 100% unique form of charisma, just like our two case studies.

Making that essence shine bright is just a matter of using the 5 traits we've identified. In a journal or word processor, answer the following questions:

Trait 1: Likeability and warmth

On a scale of 1 to 10, how warm and likeable are you, honestly?

What single behavior can you identify as an obstacle to you being more likable?

Think of times in the past where you've felt really warm, kind, and benevolent – what was happening, and what made it so easy to broadcast your friendliness in that moment?

Can you identify a single person who you could be warmer and kinder to? How?

Trait 2: Power and influence

Do you have a clear mission, passion or project in life you care deeply about?

If so, does everyone in your world clearly know about it?

Being honest, do you know your own value? Do other people? Why or why not?

What is holding you back from "speaking your truth" right now? What might be the costs of not speaking up about what you believe in?

Trait 3: Emotional intelligence

Think of the last time you felt you connected emotionally with someone. What were they doing, and what were you doing?

Thinking deeply, what is the thing you most want from others when you engage with them? Attention? Validation? Distraction? Stimulation?

What can you do *today* to gift this feeling to someone in your own world?

Trait 4: Presence, awareness and self-control

To what extent do you plan and prepare for social interactions?

According to your values and goals, how would you most like to come across to those around you?

Do you know how others see you? How could you find out?

What is the one thing you could do right now to communicate your ideal persona to others?

Trait 5: Social intelligence and leadership

What unique insights and abilities do you possess that nobody else does?

Are you conveying those to the world? If not, how could you start?

What would you like to create around you if you had infinite power and influence?

What small step can you take right now towards that vision?

Finally, to bring it all together:

What does your ultimate, supremely charismatic alter ego look like? What do they say, and how do they act?

What are your biggest flaws and weakness in social interactions? How would your alter ego deal with these?

Are you a larger-than-life extroverted and sparkly charismatic, or do you have a more a magnetic, alluring and introverted presence?

Think of the people you most admire for their charisma – what could you easily do right now to mimic some of their behavior?

Which questions were hardest to answer, and why do you think that is?

Finally, warmth, influence, presence, etc..... which aspects of charisma are most natural for you, and which are you happy to leave less developed?

To be frank, many of us have an internal picture of who we are and how we like to see ourselves, but this is often a lot more flattering than how other people actually see us! As you work at cultivating the kind of charismatic aura that fits you best, be prepared to be honest with yourself and admit when something isn't working. You could be a completely amazing person, but if you are not communicating that properly, it almost doesn't matter.

It's our responsibility to know where we stand and to take steps to improve. The above questions are a good start, but they need to be made real in the world through concrete action. Today (right now, when you finish reading this chapter!), commit to taking one small step, whether that's smiling at someone in the street, striking up a conversation with a stranger, or hitting the gym, so you feel more comfortable and confident in your own body.

Summary

- We can condense the four theories of charisma into 5 distinct charismatic traits: likeability and warmth; power and influence; emotional intelligence; presence, awareness and self-control; and social intelligence and leadership. If we can consistently hit these five notes in our social interactions, we cannot help but boost our "charisma quotient."
- To be impactful, charisma has to be genuine to us. We need to take responsibility for honestly appraising our skills and taking concrete action to improve in real life. Whether we are

extroverted or introverted, there is a unique charisma style that will work for us.

- Real life celebrities and historical figures can serve as examples and inspiration. Both Will Smith and Marilyn Monroe show how you can tick all 5 charisma boxes, but in completely different ways.

- Will Smith teaches us to be prepared, stay humble and work hard, and lead with positivity, humor, and good-naturedness. Though his social mask makes him appear easygoing and lighthearted, it conceals the effort, deliberation and hard work required to build the life and image you want.

- Marilyn Monroe teaches us that charisma can also be about magnetically drawing people towards you, rather than being loud and over the top to demand attention. Marilyn shows us the power of appearance, and how to craft a performing person down to the finest detail. She also shows us indirectly that perfection is not required, and that if you can lean honestly into your own vulnerability and fragility, people may love you all the more for it.

- You can design your own unique charisma formula by honestly rating how you perform in each of these five areas, and committing to taking action today to improve.

Part 2: Creating Charismatic Interactions

Chapter 4: The bedrock of good communication

In part 1, we looked at clear definitions for what charisma actually is, as well as explored four different models or theories about what charisma is made of, and how to increase each of these aspects in ourselves. With consistent practice smiling, being present, adjusting body language, conveying warmth, and so on, we can cultivate our own unique, charismatic aura that people can't help but feel when they're in our presence.

In part 2, we take this carefully cultivated aura and further extend it to others in social interactions. Just as we are in charge of the persona we broadcast to others, we also have a degree of control over how interactions play out. With a little know-how, we can learn to create moments, conversations, and connections that really sparkle. Charisma *in action* is not all that different from being a scintillating conversationalist, a good listener, a witty storyteller or an empathetic friend. In other words, it's impossible to be charismatic without exceptional communication skills.

In the following chapters, we'll look at simple and straightforward ways to be a better listener, master small talk, read people's emotions and engage authentically with people. But all of this stems from a more fundamental skill, without which none of it can happen: empathy.

Empathy is so, so much more than feeling for others when something bad happens to them. Empathy is really the only thing that allows human beings to reach out and connect to one another emotionally. Without empathy we cannot imagine another person's world, perspective, or emotions. Philosophers call this capacity to guess at the hidden inner world of people other than ourselves "theory of mind." In imagining another's inner world, empathy is the *what*, and communication is the *how*. If we want to connect emotionally with others and share in their world, we need to understand how to communicate with them. If there isn't empathy, other people are nothing more than abstract entities to us, rather than living, breathing beings that we can *feel*.

There are actually two kinds of empathy: positive and negative. A charismatic person has both. Picture a woman who wins last place at a beauty pageant. She smiles broadly, hugs the winner and congratulates her. She revels in the winner's excitement and takes pleasure in her happiness, telling her how proud she is of her. It's a good look, right? This is what is called positive empathy – the ability to derive joy from other people's joy, and to feel good purely because they do. This is not even about social self-control, but genuine pleasure at other people's fortunes.

It's the opposite of jealousy, insecurity and selfishness, because it centers and finds satisfaction in someone else. The irony is that it ends up making the admirer so much more likeable, too! Charismatic people are never jealous (at least not outwardly...), and they don't compete in public or put themselves or others down. Watch any interview with the charismatic Dolly Parton, for example, and observe how she never puts down others in the industry, even those who criticize her. She playfully laughs off even insults with grace and humor. "I'm not offended by all the dumb blonde jokes because I know I'm not dumb – I also know I'm not blonde."

You can improve your own charisma by refusing to let other people's achievements threaten you, or their light undermine your own. Anxious people take the brilliance of others as a problem, perhaps because deep down, they doubt themselves and feel insecure. But if you get alongside those who are doing better than you, you elevate yourself and communicate a powerful message that you know how to generate your own value *that does not depend on others being smaller than you*.

When you feel that tinge of jealousy or envy, swallow your pride and praise or congratulate that person. Ask for their advice. Lavish them with compliments. Be their friend. See if you can genuinely find happiness for them. This not only makes you appear more magnanimous and mature as a person, but it will encourage you to think: why don't I do the same? Train yourself to see jealousy as an invitation to be better. Is there some potential going unfulfilled in you?

Negative empathy is the one most of us are familiar with, i.e., the ability to sympathize with and feel into the pain and suffering of others. Being able to help, support and comfort those in need is great, but it usually comes from a deeper ability to sincerely feel what others feel. Intellectually understanding the facts of someone's negative emotion is not the same as *feeling* that emotion along with them.

So how do improve empathy? That's easy! Empathy is hard-wired in almost everybody; it's just a question of consciously bringing out this innate ability in every interaction. In a 2013 paper by Klimecki et al., researchers discovered that empathy is plastic, meaning it can literally be cultivated with effort. Even if you find empathy difficult or have trouble empathizing with particular people, it doesn't matter; there are still predictable patterns of empathetic conversation that anyone can learn to demonstrate. Fake it until you make it, in other words!

Strategy 1: Read

It might seem odd that this solitary activity would make you more socially charismatic and better in conversations – but it does!

Reading puts you in someone else's shoes. You get to try on perspectives other than your own, inhabit someone else's narrative, see their values, and feel their interpretation of events. Think of it as an empathy training camp.

When you're with others, try to really grasp that from their point of view, they are the most important people in their worlds, in the same way that you feel that you are the center of your own. You begin to build real empathy when you understand that other people will always experience themselves as the protagonists of a story that may run on values and principles completely alien to you. And you can tailor and adjust your communication accordingly.

A kind and sympathetic person can think, "I feel for you, because I'd feel bad if that happened to *me*." But a truly empathetic person can think, "I feel for you, because I can see that it feels bad for *you*." Reading fiction helps you appreciate others, and see them not from your perspective, but see them how they see themselves, from their perspective. Make sure it's the right kind of reading though – mix up your authors and go for quality literary fiction from different eras, countries and styles to broaden your scope. Reading the same author constantly or flipping through People magazine doesn't count...

Strategy 2: Make an experience filter

You know how in kid's TV shows, the hero occasionally says something like, "now, if I were a lost walrus who escaped from a zoo, where is the first place I would go?" It sounds silly, but the ability to genuinely see life through the lens of someone (or some walrus) who isn't you is actually a sophisticated expression of empathy – and helps us be charismatic.

Try this right now: think of someone you're very close to, and then think of a current situation or issue in your own life. Now, ask yourself, "what would X think or feel about this situation?" Literally pretend you are them, with all their idiosyncrasies, beliefs, blind spots, goals and fears. When you do this, you create an "experience filter" that acts as a representation of that person in your mind. It's not the same as that person, no, but it is a stepping stone that helps you get into their world and empathize, as well as see the limits of your own perspective.

People react to life and interpret situations according to who they are. If you can really *see* this, you give yourself an edge in any social interaction. You can pitch your communication to them so that they actually hear it. For example, maybe you're a very emotional and verbally expressive person, but you know your mechanical engineer friend is more of a concrete, visual person who thinks in practical terms.

When you want to ask for their help, you don't get too focused on your vision of things, and instead frame your request as they would: you appeal to their logical side, and ask briefly for a clear and limited set of actions, focusing not on how grateful you'd be to get their help, but how it makes sense to ask them since they're the most knowledgeable, and the problem needs to be solved. When you hear people say about others that they "can talk to anyone," this is what they mean: a charismatic person doesn't just know how to speak, they know how to speak *other people's languages*.

Strategy 3: Deliberately practice theory of mind

Let's say you're at the post office and trying to get a package mailed, but the person behind the counter is being *really* unhelpful. You're in a rush and they're apparently not, and all you can focus on is the way the interaction feels to you: this person is standing in the way of the thing you want, and it's beginning to get annoying. Perhaps you look at their actions – the dawdling, the "attitude" or the refusal to quickly cut a few corners to speed things up – and from your perspective it looks like they're being obtuse and stubborn. You say rudely, "are you *trying* to make me angry?"

A little empathy could go a long way in a situation like this. Empathy could help us understand other people's behavior not in relation to our own interpretations, goals or values, but according to theirs. Empathy could make us peak out of our experience and into someone else's. It could help us notice, for example, that we are the last customer of the day, and that the post office was due to close 5 minutes ago. You might notice that the person is taking a long time because they have to boot the system back up again. What does the situation look like from their perspective? Just a few moments pondering this, and we'd have a novel insight: the person believes they're already doing us a favor after a long day by agreeing to serve us past closing time. From their point of view, *we* are the rude ones.

Theory of mind allows us to have the mature and grounding realization that we are not the only ones in the universe, and that our point of view is just that: a point of view, not reality itself. Everything other people say and do comes from a perfectly legitimate perspective informed by their background and their unique take on things. Our own thoughts, attitudes, expectations and interpretations might feel invisible to us, but they are no less arbitrary than anyone else's. Without theory of mind, we barge ahead on our own mission, insensitive to other people's realities. The result is usually conflict, misunderstanding or, even at the best of times, a failure to connect.

Deliberately practicing theory of mind doesn't mean focusing on other people's perspectives to the exclusion of your own. It simply means being aware that there are different viewpoints in the first place! Many of unconsciously place ourselves at the center of every conversation, and assume that others share our desires, know what we know, and think as we think. When you stop doing this, you naturally become more accepting and open-minded, because you no longer privilege your own experience as somehow more central or important than others'.

Here's a trick to try next time you find yourself thinking that someone is confusing, infuriating or plain old wrong. *Assume that their behavior makes total sense.* Take as a given that their words and actions completely align with their perspective, and then ask what that tells you about that perspective.

The way we ourselves act always makes sense to us because we know what is happening inside our own minds (usually!). But when someone behaves in a way that gets to us, it can be extremely useful to ask, "what does this behavior tell me about this person's perspective?" From that point on, you can talk to that perspective, rather than to a strawman or reflection of your own perspective. You're also likely to respect and accept that viewpoint, rather than seeing it as a problem simply because it's not like yours.

Strategy 4: Listen for facts versus interpretations

A great way to build more empathy and get into people's perspectives is to practice listening to what you're told, and discerning between fact and opinion. This is more difficult than it first seems. In conversations, perspective, interpretation, opinion and unique points of view are often presented mixed with concrete facts. The facts are just facts – the capital of Italy is Rome, today is Tuesday, your car has four wheels – but everything else is up for discussion. When people talk, they're really offering you a sprinkle of fact... and a big mix of assumptions, interpretations, expectations, beliefs, anecdotal memories, arguments, value judgments and claims. This is where perspective lives. Change any of these, and the perspective changes, too.

Imagine someone says to you, "Last Tuesday, the guy at the post office lost his temper with me completely out of the blue." Let's look closely at this. What is fact here? Well, the person was at the post office last Tuesday. There was a guy there. And everything else? Not fact. That someone "lost their temper" is value judgment and interpretation. "Out of the blue" is an opinion and personal assessment.

Basically, there are many unknowns here, and only a few facts. Maybe it was *not* out of the blue, but completely warranted. Maybe no tempers were lost, but there was simply some mild irritation. And maybe the irritation was not directed at the person speaking, but the result of something entirely unrelated. By separating out fact from fiction this way, you are clearly identifying what the person's perspective is: from their point of view, this is the story. However, simply changing the words of the story allows you to realize this perspective is at play and then switch it up. "Lost his temper" could be reworded as "yelled at the top of his lungs" or "got a little impatient", each framing a different perspective.

The true value here is that you can read between the lines and understand their emotions and what it is that they are really trying to express. Usually, it's not the facts or logic, it's the emotions. Anyone that has ever had an argument with a significant other can attest to this; logic will only get you so far because the reason there is an argument in the first place is almost always due to underlying emotions not being attended to or heard. When you know the difference between facts and interpretation, you will know what to focus on and make people feel glad that they told you something – because you can give them the reaction they were looking for instead of blindly focusing on pedantry.

All of this is to say that if you want to master perspective-switching and having the empathy needed for real charisma, you need to learn to identify the language of a perspective, as well as change that language to change perspective. Charismatic people know that words are like magic – when you change them, the whole world seems to change before your eyes. This understanding allows a charismatic person to say to the post office worker, "Gosh! You're such a lifesaver helping me out last minute like this. Thank you for being so quick!"

The postal worker feels seen, understood and maybe a little flattered. From their perspective, they also want to get things done as quickly as possible. They work as fast as they humanly can and are polite, too – which is not the outcome you'd get if you'd impatiently asked, "what's the hold up anyway?"

Summary

- Part 1 of this book is all about the charismatic presence. How might you wish for someone to describe you, and how much does that differ from reality? And

112

then, how do you bridge the gap between these two versions of yourself? Part 1 is more theoretical and introspective, while Part 2 is all about action. How do you actually create the type of interactions that will draw people to you, regardless of your current personality?

- Unsurprisingly, it all starts with empathy. When you have empathy, you know what other people are thinking and feeling, or at least you can make a pretty darned good guess about it. And if we know what people are thinking and feeling, we can also make a darned good guess as to what they want. And that's what will allow us to create charismatic interactions.

- The first is to simply read more. This is probably the best practice you can do without having someone in front of you, because it forces you to inhabit someone else's perspective and inner dialogue. You can see in the story that because X happened, Y and Z might happen. This seems simple, but it is not easy to practice in daily life. Having an experience filter is very similar, in that it forces you to step out of your perspective (which is necessarily limited) and really try to see someone else's. It might sound like we are only talking about empathy here, but the truth is that empathy and charisma are extremely, extremely related. Yes, deliberately practicing theory of mind is also more in the same direction of understanding another person's thoughts and emotions.

- Finally, understanding the difference between facts and interpretation will help you know what you should respond to. Almost always, you should be trying to respond to people's interpretation because their emotions are buried within, and that's what will draw people to you.

Chapter 5: Engaging Fully

Questions – An Underrated Superpower

The physicist and theorist Heisenberg famously said, "What we observe is not nature itself, but nature exposed to our method of questioning." In the realm of conversation, we can take this to mean that what we see when we engage with other people is not how they really are, but how they look in relation to how we talk to them, and the questions we pose. To put it bluntly, if you ask boring questions, you get boring answers. If you don't ask *any* questions—well, the person in front of you starts to look like nothing more than a blank.

With all this focus on our own mindset, our preparedness and our ability to set the mood, we can forget that we always have at hand a very effective technique for reaching others—just ask them! Questions initiate and move conversations along particular paths. They give you some control and direction, they help you show interest, and they help you genuinely connect to and understand the person in front of you. In fact, questions are so important that it's hard to imagine anyone getting far in conversations without them.

Here, we'll focus on the *emotional* rather than *informational* impact of questions. You are not asking someone something because you literally don't know the answer and want them to tell you. That's what Google is for. In that sense, the answer can be important, sure, but it's not all that's important Simply asking in the first place, and the way you ask, can also send a powerful message. This chapter is about participating fully in conversations, and the backbone of quality participation is to think like a scientist like Heisenberg, and *get curious*.

The first thing to understand: not all questions are created equally. We can group exchanges, and therefore questions, into three levels, according to their underlying purpose. The first is to exchange information (or learn), the second to exchange feelings and emotions (or get others to bond with and like us), and the third is to exchange values (ditto). It's worth knowing the difference, so you're clear on what kind of conversation you're having, and why. For example, the know-it-all from our first chapter makes a mistake in responding to other people's appeals for an exchange of emotion and feelings, by supplying factual information instead. This is the person who completely misses the point by focusing on the details and not shared emotional content.

The second thing to understand is that we need to master both the asking and the answering of questions, at the right level. Doing so makes us more likeable, more empathetic, and more successfully at connecting to others. Let's take a closer look at how to frame and interpret questions, to use them to their best advantage.

Just ask more. Chances are, you're simply not asking enough questions. Even emotionally intelligent people can fail to show enough curiosity for others. Maybe you're too busy thinking of yourself or stressed about the interaction (still egocentric!) or maybe you genuinely don't care enough to know the answer. Maybe you think questions make you look nosy or worse, unsure of yourself. But the opposite is true.

Harvard research by Alison Wood Brooks and colleagues showed that when people were instructed to ask more questions in a conversation, people rated them as more likable than those who asked fewer questions. Speed daters were also found to agree more readily to a second date if their first date was filled with plenty of questions.

Don't be worried about coming off badly; the truth is that questions unlock the next level of human connection, and may even be more powerful in situations where questions are *not* expected, such as job interviews. They show that you're paying attention, that you care, that you're engaging in the situation proactively, that you have your own values and expectations, that you appreciate the opinion of the other person (otherwise, you wouldn't be asking for it) and that you have been listening. Not bad for a single line!

The Socratic Method

The kind of questions and the way they're delivered matters, of course. And, unfortunately, it's not just up to you how well the conversation goes—the other party has to be on board, too. There might be a person who asks a lot of questions paired with someone who asks none, or a pair where both ask a lot, or a pair where neither do. Each of these dynamics is going to feel different.

The main reason is that each person may share different conversational goals. If both parties have the goal of connecting and getting something done together, the atmosphere will be cooperative. If one or both parties is using the conversation to gain an upper hand, wheedle out information or boast, the interaction becomes competitive. If one or both have very minimal goals for the conversation, it may just fizzle out, and so on.

Understanding that people are coming from different places when they talk to one another helps you in two ways: firstly, you can identify what kind of conversation you're in. If you're stuck with someone hellbent on competition and grandstanding, there may be little you can do but be polite and find a way to exit, or at the least refrain from sharing any information that would put you at a disadvantage. On the other hand, knowing the kind of exchange you *want* to be in can help you actively cerate it with others.

Use follow-up questions. Questions are good, but follow-up questions are better, because they show you were listening, and care enough to keep learning more. Good follow-up questions zone in on an important fact the other person has just shared—if you simply spout off a string of unconnected questions it may feel like an interrogation. But run with what's already been said and you tap into the conversation's momentum and flow.

Use open-ended questions. The idea is that you genuinely want to learn more, so don't go in with a very specific question that puts the other person on the spot or makes it seem like you're only after a particular response. Avoid yes/no questions or leading questions ("So, what do like best about our glorious leader?"). You don't people to feel as though your questions are there simply to extract sensitive information out of you, since this will cause them to clam up or distrust you—rightly!

Use questions to break the ice—gently. It may seem counterintuitive, but if you are curious about something, coming out and asking straight away can help cut through awkwardness faster than beating around the bush. You just have to do it right. No, you don't want to offend people or make them uncomfortable, but a well-pitched question can have an interesting effect—people may feel that you are so curious and interested in their answer that you are willing to gently bend social etiquette. Most people find this flattering! At the very least, you can mask potentially nosy seeming questions with a little humor. Another idea is to proceed your question with a bit of sharing on your part, as though to communicate nonverbally, "I'll show you mine if you show me yours!"

Here's an example of these kinds of questions in action. Picture a quick break room conversation with the new recruit at work. They're a little shy, but you push on and take your chance to start a conversation while you wait for your coffee to brew.

You: "Oh, hi there! You're the new hire in accounting, right?"

Them: "Yup. It's my first day."

You: "Oh, awesome. They're starting you off easy, I hope?" (A gentle question to gauge reaction only.)

Them: "Haha, yeah, I guess. I'm heading to IT right now to get my access code sorted out."

You: "Go on, be honest, what do you think about our state-of-the-art break room? I love working here but me and this microwave do *not* get on." (Breaking the ice, asking emotional/feeling questions rather than dwelling on the facts of what they're up to in the accounting department. Plus, a playful complaint is hard not to respond to.)

Them: "Oh, it's not so bad! You should see mine at home. I think its suicidal, actually."

You: "Ah, great, so you have experience with depressed appliances; you'll fit right in. So, you said you're on your way to IT. Have you met Rob yet?" (Follow-up question.)

Them: "Rob? I don't think so . . ."

You: "Rob's great, you'll love him. I've got to go, but good luck with your microwave! Hey, I should ask, do you live locally? The commute's out here can be hell . . ." (Another follow-up question.)

Them: "Oh yeah, I'm just down the road, in [wherever]."

You: Oh, cool. You should come hang out with some of us on Fridays. We meet up at the bar on the corner . . ."

. . . and so on.

In this conversation, questions are helping everything flow more easily and comfortably. They all seem natural and good-natured, and likely make the new recruit feel respected and paid attention to. In just a two-minute exchange, a great impression is made.

When asking questions, be casual, take your lead from others, and pay attention to group dynamics. Mix up the kinds of questions you ask, but always be mindful about the match between you—are you sharing information, feelings, or values? Respond accordingly, or be prepared to gently try shift the frame with your question.

"Hey, how's it going?" (If said quickly and carelessly, not really a question, just polite conversational protocol—a similarly offhand question or response is probably enough.)

"So you were just released from prison?" (A request for information—possibly more, but this person likely wants to know the precise factual answer.)

"What do you think about the blue? The red looks better doesn't it?" (This is not a request for information—blue or red is irrelevant. The person is unsure which to choose and needs reassurance, or for you to share your own opinion. This is a request for an emotional response.)

"Where do you see our relationship going?" (A request not just for feelings, but broader values, such as whether marriage is important to them. If someone simply responds with how they're feeling right now, it's likely not going to be perceived as a satisfying or complete answer.)

What about when you respond to questions? As we've seen, it's a good idea to be open, and give more information than was asked for. Take your time in answering. Listen for what the person is actually looking for from you— are they just passing the time and being polite, or do they genuinely want to know more? Adjust your answer accordingly.

The Conversational Narcissism Ratio

Have you ever quietly waited for someone to stop speaking, thinking all the while about what you would say the moment they shut up? If so, you've likely been guilty of conversational narcissism! It is the inability to put aside your own internal monologue completely, and focus on what the other person is thinking or saying. It leads to the same outcome of dueling monologues, where conversation hasn't really happened at all— rather, you have two people talking *at* each other instead of *with* each other.

It's also a big reason why people fail to ask questions—or listen properly to their answers.

So, to start with, improve your listening skills by being vigilant about the ways in which craving attention can make you a worse conversationalist. This takes some conscious awareness and also a little honesty. We can ask what our true intentions and motivations are for entering into conversations, in general and specifically with people we know. Are we reaching out to others because we want the validation of their attention? Because we want the feeling of proving ourselves right and another wrong? Because we feel we have to for some reason?

Do we see conversation as a battle, or a game, or a dance? Perhaps we see conversation as an opportunity to show ourselves off, or share what interests us. Whatever your reasons are, though, you probably notice that they usually concern only *you* . . . and don't spare a thought for the other person sharing the conversation with you! How many of us can honestly say that our goal is to see and understand the other person, rather than just to have ourselves seen and understood?

The idea is not to always seek to turn attention to yourself. Conversations should be thought of not as a means to win attention, but to *share* it enjoyably with someone else. The goal is not competition for the floor, but cooperation with an ally. The purpose is to collaborate, not express solely. The aim is to learn, not teach, and so on. For some of us, this may require a complete re-tooling of what we seek when we want to be social.

After an ineffective conversation, people may feel depleted, bored, or even more alone. Good conversations, on the other hand, can be things of beauty, allowing both participants to create between them something bigger than the sum of its parts. One study even discovered that people valued being listened to and heard so much that, in an experiment, were actually willing to pay to enjoy the feeling. That's because that feeling of being acknowledged, heard and respected is incredibly valuable. Offering that feeling to someone else is just as rewarding, if not more so, than experiencing it for yourself. The truth is that if you prioritize the other person in this way, you often end up with a mutually fulfilling conversation anyway, without actually trying.

Listening well requires that you suspend your own self-interest and ego and gracefully allow someone else to shine.

It's now time to get self-conscious and introspective. Sociologist Charles Derber has studied this phenomenon extensively and believes that this form of conversational narcissism can occur without people even being aware it's going on. It can be easy to imagine that conversational narcissists are the stereotypical loudmouths who dominate conversation—but it's far subtler than this. It turns out that the situation can turn on a single word choice. He articulated what he called *support responses* and *shift responses*, and how they can subtly pervade our everyday vocabulary.

Derber explains what he calls "initiatives" in conversation—which can be *attention giving* or *attention seeking*, the latter of which can be further divided into active or passive. This is a little like our tennis analogy—in tennis, we are always either returning the ball or receiving it from the other player, enacting a give and take. In a conversation, what moves back and forth is awareness and attention. These can bounce between people, or pool on one side of the conversation. For our purposes, you can guess which kinds of behaviors we want to orient toward. Let's look at some examples of both in conversation.

Let's first look at support responses, which are what they sound like: words or behaviors that support the expression of the other person in the conversation. For the active, attention-giving variety, a "*support response*" maintains attention on the speaker and their topic—for example, asking a question about what's been said. Support responses can be simple acknowledgements ("Oh really?" "Uh huh."), positively supporting ("That's great!"), or in question form ("What did you say then?"). You can imagine the other person's story is a balloon that everyone else is trying to keep aloft, jumping in here and there to bounce it back up into the air. For instance:

"I love French films."

Response: "Which is your favorite?"

The above response only exists to maintain attention and awareness on the original speaker. The response doesn't interject any new information of its own, but encourages the flow of attention already unfolding. Obviously, this can make people feel, well, supported! This is a great way to validate your conversation partner, let them know you're listening, and send a strong message that you value what they're saying and want to hear more.

The "*shift response*," however, is an active attention-seeking response that shifts the attention to the other person, in other words back to themselves. It's an act of grabbing the spotlight and pointing it in the opposite direction. With a shift response, the flow of attention and awareness is suddenly diverted elsewhere. What's going on when you see two people vying for attention and talking over one another? Their dialogue is made exclusively of aggressive shift responses!

"I love French films."

Response: "Yeah? I've never cared much about movies. The other day, actually, I saw this thing at the cinema . . ."

This isn't to say that shift responses are always wrong—in context, they can work, especially if the other person subtly reclaims attention again. Sometimes it might even behoove you to use more shift responses to grab some of the spotlight, or make your feelings known. But how much are you using them?

A shift response is a great idea if you want to move the chat along to another topic, or inject some fresh energy or ideas into the conversation. It's a bad idea if you are simply trying to derail the existing conversation in your favor, so you can say what you want to say. Many people get together and talk this way, each announcing a different personal anecdote that begins with a shift response.

If you have two people with poor listening skills, and both are hell-bent on shift responses, you end up with a wrestling match for attention, rather than a conversation. Maybe both parties are satisfying their lust for expression, but their gas tanks for being heard are running on empty. You may not notice if you are locked in this type of battle, but from the outside looking in, observing this kind of interaction can be curious and confusing.

Moreover, if a bad conversationalist (someone who continually uses shift responses) is paired with a very empathetic listener (someone who continually uses support responses), one party may well feel as though they're having a good talk because the other person is consistently offering them support responses, while that person actually wants to jump off a bridge because the conversation is turning into an awkward pseudo-lecture on the other person's life and beliefs.

What about passive conversational narcissism? Naturally, some people are still quite aware of social norms and etiquette and so will vie for attention in subtler ways. One way of doing this is to fail to offer support responses, waiting till the other person's thread dies away and you can take the limelight. Here, you are hoping that the other person runs out of steam so you can finally get your word in. It is like sitting in a tree and waiting for the prey to get tired and go to sleep—you know it will happen eventually, so you passively bide your time.

Have you been part of a conversation where the other person didn't offer any support responses, even a quaint "Oh really?" or "Uh-huh"? You're not quite sure whether they've taken in what you've said, and that may be intentional on their part. It may have been a case of passive conversational narcissism. It's like letting that balloon drop to the floor. You don't have to do much to make someone else feel that what they're saying hasn't really "landed"!

Most of us are taught that it's polite to not ramble on, to take your turn and then rest, and to share space in conversations. Fine, this person will follow those basic rules. But they sure won't encourage their conversation partner to speak more, lest it cut into their own speaking time! A lack of (genuine!) feedback from the other person can quickly make someone feel they ought to stop speaking—and this is where the conversational narcissist steps back into the picture.

Though it's tempting to try to catch other people in the act of conversational narcissism, its far more productive to learn to notice it in *yourself* and guard against it. You can't control what others do, but you can control your actions and how good of a listener you are. After all, that is the goal of this book. For the other purpose, you may want to seek a book on persuasion or hypnosis.

The irony is it's often those who are able to listen well, to step aside, and to take a genuine interest in their conversation partners who become people we think of as most interesting, charismatic and worthy of our attention in the first place. So the purported goal of conversational narcissism (*making darn sure that people know things about you*) isn't even satisfied. Oops. Luckily, there are a few guidelines to battle these unconscious obstacles you'll undoubtedly face.

Balance your needs and desires with other people's.

To do this, you first need to be aware of your focus and where it's going. Pay attention to how the airtime is being distributed. Is one person doing all the talking? Is there a back-and-forth? This requires more than just playing at being interested in another person's life—you genuinely need to forget yourself for a moment and engage fully, and honestly, in what someone else is saying. Stop thinking about your response for the future, and pay attention to what someone is currently saying to you.

This means no rushing in to explain or frame what they've said so that it relates back to you again. Give more supportive responses, and guard against constantly referring every topic back to yourself. Ask questions to invite the other person to say more. If you take attention for a while, enjoy it—but volley it back again. Like we were taught as children: It's good to share!

"As you were talking, it made me think about this experience I had once, where XYZ. That made me wonder, did you find that XYZ was the case as well?" A person saying this demonstrates that they're willing to share the conversation, rather than hog it all for themselves.

Think about ego, power, self-esteem, and control.

Those who seem most boastful in a conversation, who jealously guard attention or speak over others, are often those who feel most insecure in themselves. Their need to control the conversation comes from a hunger for attention and approval. If you find yourself using conversations as a platform to boost your ego, feel better about yourself, or be witnessed and supported by others, your work may be to learn to be comfortable taking the back seat for a change. The paradox is that people who seem most likeable and confident are those who don't appear to be making frantic efforts to dominate others' attention.

What Would Conan Do and Curiosity

Let's return to an idea we touched on earlier—the idea of playfulness and curiosity in conversation. Curiosity plays a huge role in the way we receive others and thus how they receive us. You can be the most charming, funniest person in the room, but if you aren't *interested and curious* about the person across from you, there simply won't be a connection. Why would there be? It's more like a one-man show than a conversation. Big surprise, it turns out that we care if the person across from us is engaged or scanning the room behind us and looking for someone better to talk to.

Staying curious is a difficult proposition because, at first glance, most people might seem uninteresting or unworthy of paying attention to. This is harsh, but it is in fact behind a lot of people's reason for "hating small talk." This is undoubtedly the biggest hurdle for most of us—even if you don't consciously think it, you subconsciously believe that someone is simply not worth being curious about. You think that even if you dig deeper you won't find anything worth your time, so why bother in the first place?

It's true that, at first glance, very few of us are compelling. You included. But acting on this impulse will limit your communication and keep you right where you are. We are cutting off people's *ability* to be interesting and compelling because we don't give them a chance. In the end, it doesn't particularly matter what you believe. Just start to build the habit of curiosity, and eventually it won't matter if you think people are worthy or not (they are). You'll be able to find the interesting aspects in just about anyone, and that's what counts.

To do so, I've found that the absolute best mindset to emulate is that of a talk show host—Jimmy Fallon, Jimmy Kimmel, Conan O'Brien, whoever your favorite is, they all do the same thing. Just ask yourself what they would do if you're struggling for what curiosity looks like and how you can wield it. Conan O'Brien happens to my favorite, so let's think about the traits he embodies in a conversation with a guest on his show.

Visualize his studio. He's got a big open space, and he is seated at a desk. His guest is seated at a chair adjacent to the desk, and it's literally like they exist in a world of their own. When Conan has a guest on his show, that guest is the center of his world for the next ten minutes. They are the most interesting person he has ever come across, everything they say is spellbinding, he is insatiably curious about their stories, and he reacts to anything they say with an uproarious laugh and an otherwise exaggerated reaction that they were seeking. He is charmingly positive and can always find a humorous spin on a negative aspect of a story.

His sole purpose is to make his guest comfortable on the show, encourage them to talk about themselves, and ultimately make them feel good and look good. In turn, this makes them share revealing things they might not otherwise share and create a connection and chemistry with him that is so important for a talk show. The viewers at home are desperate to learn about this celebrity guest, so Conan acts as a proxy for their curiosity. Also, the viewers can tell in an instant if either party is mailing it in or faking it, so Conan's job literally depends on his ability to use his curiosity to connect on a deeper level.

Even with grumpy or more quiet guests, he is able to elevate their energy levels and attitudes simply by being intensely interested in them (at an energy level slightly above theirs) and encouraging them by giving them the great reactions that they seek. It's almost as if he plays the game "How little can I say to get the most out of people?" It's a non-obvious talent that is worth its weight in gold—and it'll make the person receive this attention feel like solid gold!

Of course, in your life, you may be faced with those people that are like pulling teeth to talk to. A little bit of friendly encouragement and affirmation can make even the meekest clam open up. Numerous questions, directing the conversation toward them, and the feeling that you actually care are also integral. Imagine the relief you can create at dreaded networking events. People like those who like them, so when you react the way they want, it encourages them to be more outgoing and open with you.

Other talk show hosts would later go on the record lamenting how often they disliked his guests and how boring he found the actors and actresses that he would be forced to speak to. But the fact that this is never really detected is a testament to how highly trained his habit of curiosity was. He started by making a conscious decision to be curious, built the habit, and engaged his guests easily; do you think his guests could tell if he was interested or not? Never.

Curiosity allows people to feel comfortable enough to speak freely beyond a superficial level—because you are demonstrating that you care and that you will listen when they open up. People won't be inclined to reveal their secret thoughts if they think it will be met with apathy, after all. So whether you have to fake it till you make it, Conan O'Brien is who your mindset and attitude should feel like.

It's a banal and often-used quote, but for good reason. Dale Carnegie said it best: "You can make more friends in two months by becoming truly interested in other people than you can in two years by trying to get other people interested in you."

In case Conan O'Brien's curiosity still isn't coming naturally to you, here are some more specific patterns of thought you can use to improve your people skills.

I wonder what they are like? When you start to wonder about the other person, it changes your perspective on them completely. This is an inkling of curiosity. You start to care about them—not only about their shallow traits, such as their occupation or how their day is going, but what motivates them and what makes them act in the way they do.

Having a sense of wonder about someone is one of the most powerful mindsets you can have because it makes you want to scratch your itch. Scratching the itch of curiosity will become secondary to everything else because you simply want to know about the other person. Here, you don't have to *like* them, exactly—it goes deeper than that. Just perceive them, as much of them as you possibly can, and genuinely allow yourself to be amazed by that.

Suppose you had a sense of wonder about computers as a child. You were probably irritating with how many questions you asked anyone that seemed to have knowledge about computers. What kind of attention span are you going to devote to computers, and what kind of questions are you going to ask? You are going to skip the small talk interview questions and get right down to the details because it's what you care and wonder about.

Keeping the mindset of wonderment will completely change the way you interact with people because you will suddenly care, and much of the time, we don't notice that we don't care about the person we are talking to. You'll dig deeper and deeper until you can put together a picture of what you are wondering about.

It's important to note here that you need to be sincere about it. Conan is a pro who gets a salary from the job he does, but for the rest of us, it's so much better to foster a genuine interest in others rather than fake it. That boring person you're chatting to? Challenge yourself and your assumptions about them. They have a history, secrets, hopes, dreams, unexpected talents—what are they?

What can they teach me? Don't read this from the perspective of attempting to gain what you can from someone. Read it from the perspective of seeing others as being people worthy of your attention. Everyone has valuable knowledge, whether it applies to your life or not. Everyone is great at something, and everyone is a domain expert in something that you are not, no matter how small or obscure. People's perspectives have innate value, and just by learning about them, we are enriched.

The main point is to ignite an interest in the other person as opposed to an apathetic approach. Imagine if you were a huge skiing junkie and you met someone that used to be a professional skier. They may have even reached the Olympics in their prime.

What will follow? You'll be thrilled by what you can potentially learn and gain from the other person, and that will guide the entire interaction. Again, there will be a level of interest and engagement if you view others as worthy of talking to. But you'd never know unless you dug.

Whether we like to admit it or not, sometimes we feel some people are not worth our time. It's a bad habit, and this line of thinking is one of the first steps toward breaking it. *Everyone* is worth our time, but you won't be able to discover it if you don't put in the work. At the very least, most people have had interesting or noteworthy experiences in life. Become curious and you just may find that your grandma's Bungo friend was an exotic dancer during the war, that the friend you knew for twenty years has a secret passion for vintage magazines, and your work colleague actually used to be a missionary in the Congo before she had kids. Who knew!

What do we have in common? This is an investigation into the life experiences you share with someone. It instantly makes them more engaging and interesting—because we feel that they are more similar to us! It may sound a bit egotistical, but we are undoubtedly more captivated by people that share the same views and interests as us, and they us.

It may even *elevate* people, especially if we are surrounded by people different from us. For instance, if you discovered that a new stranger was born in the same hospital as you were, despite being in a different country, you would instantly feel more open to them. This person *must* share similar worldviews, values, and humor. You now have a positive bias toward them, actively seeking out more good in them.

But you wouldn't have discovered that if you didn't make an attempt at digging.

You are going to be on a hunt, and you will ask the important questions that get you where you want to be. You might jump from topic to topic, or you might dive in and ask directly.

Perhaps it's just because you will have something to fixate on besides talking for talking's sake, but these attitudes will drastically change how you approach people. Curiosity can still be hard, which is why my final suggestion for creating curiosity is to make a game of it. Your goal is to learn as much about the other person as possible. Alternatively, assume there is something extremely thrilling and exciting about the other person and make it your quest to find it. Eventually, you'll find what you're looking for.

The next time you go out to a café or store, put these attitudes to the test with the captive audience of the baristas or cashiers you come across—the lucky few who are paid to be nice to you. Do you perceive these workers to be below you, or do you treat them differently than you would treat a good friend? Do you have a sense of wonderment and curiosity about them? What do you think they can teach you, and what do you have in common with them?

Do you tend to ask the baristas or cashiers about their day and actually care about their answer? If not, do you think you'll be able to simply "turn it on" when you're around people you care about? Practice your mindsets about the people around you. It's the easiest practice you'll have because you don't have to lift a finger, but it drastically transforms the quality of relationships you'll create.

Summary

- In order to interact and engage more fully in conversations, we need to work against our not-so-useful habits and learn better ones.
- A non-negotiable habit is becoming a master at using questions. The right questions help people feel closer to us, communicate our attention and care, share our competence, show that we're aware and paying attention, deepen intimacy, guide the conversation, and make us more trustworthy.
- All exchanges, and hence all questions, are typically on one of three possible levels:

those exchanging factual information, those exchanging feelings and emotions, and those communicating deeper values. In social situations, you'll lean more heavily on the last two, but a good conversation works when people have similar conversational goals and are matched in the level they're interacting on.

- Conversational narcissism is an impediment to curiosity, engagement, and good question asking. Whether unconscious or conscious, this usually results from us placing something other than connection with the other person as our goal for conversation, i.e. to brag, to defend, to compete.

- We can reduce our own conversational narcissism by using questions. Follow-up questions are very effective, as are open-ended questions that don't make people uncomfortable, but may *gently* push on the barrier or normal etiquette.

- Just as a role model can be a guide and inspiration for your own behavior, a model can also help you stay curious when you talk to others. Talk show hosts are experts and placing their conversation partners front and center, so we can ask, what would they do? Usually, the answer is "treat my guest like the most interesting person in the whole universe."

- Curiosity needs to be genuine. We all have a bias against others sometimes, assuming they're not very interesting, but unless we ask, we won't learn about their more fascinating sides. Assume that everyone has something to teach you, and foster a genuine inquisitiveness into the details of their world. I guarantee you will not be disappointed.

Chapter 6: Subtly Charismatic

Humor and Misdirection

Phew! Time to lighten things up, wouldn't you say? Let's turn our attention to the surprisingly versatile skills of humor or its closely related cousin, misdirection. To put it simply, misdirection is when you say one thing and then proceed with an immediate opposite. For example, "It's a secret, but let me tell you immediately," or, "That show is great, except for everyone in it." It's not rolling-in-the-aisles funny, but it definitely captures attention, and gives conversation a kind of light playfulness that most people will be happy to call wit.

It seems confusing, but what you are doing is breaking a sentence into two parts.

You're stating something in the first part, then contradicting it immediately in the second. People won't immediately be sure of what you mean, and part of the humor comes from this introduced confusion. You have both positive and negative, or vice versa, in the same sentence.

The second part of the sentence is the element that people will react to, while the first part is typically the setup. The second is your true sentiment on the topic.

This formula is the secret to the humor in such lines as George Jessel's, "The human brain is a wonderful organ. It starts to work as soon as you are born and doesn't stop until you get up to deliver a speech." Douglas Adams also used it when he said, "I love deadlines. I like the whooshing sound they make as they fly by." Here's another example: "I love dogs, but I hate seeing, hearing, and touching them," or, "This juice is awesome. Did it come from the garbage disposal?"

There's just such an appealing zing to

statements like this. You can probably agree that they work, but *why* do they work?

Most of us try to be polite to people. We use euphemisms frequently, and we don't say what we really feel. The first part of a misdirecting statement is what people expect—politeness. It's you following the same old tired expected script. But then surprise! You contradict yourself and give them a dose of reality, which sets up a humorous contrast since you have deviated from what most people expect and would say themselves. As you might have observed, ironic similes also make use of misdirection to derive comedic effect. The whole effect is to send a powerful message that you don't take yourself, or the topic at hand, all that seriously. Done right, misdirection can be amazingly charming and funny—it's a way to break the rules that works so well because you appear to be using the rules at first.

Last but not least, misdirection is simply a funny way to express your feelings on something. If you really feel X about a topic, then use misdirection! "Opposite of X, but actually X," will almost always be received far better than "Gosh, I hate X."

Sarcasm is a way for people to say things without saying them, and is the most common way we use misdirection.

Think about how Chandler Bing from the television show *Friends* talks. If he says something is wonderful, he says *it's wonnnnderful* in a tone that immediately lets you know that he thinks the opposite.

Sarcasm functions like a social cue—both are ways to express something without having to explicitly say it. In that way, it's a great device for handling uncomfortable topics or pointing out the elephant in the room without directly offending people (or pointing). It allows us to walk a tightrope, as long as we don't fall into the pit of passive-aggressiveness.

At some level, most of us can appreciate sarcasm because we know what is being accomplished. It can even be the basis for your own personal brand of humor. Standup comics often use it to great effect.

Chances are, you are already using sarcasm regularly without being fully aware of it. Sarcasm is mostly used as friendly banter with a friend or acquaintance with whom you are comfortable saying something negative. For example, consider that you've committed a minor gaffe at work, for example forgetting to return a borrowed file before it's due. If a close colleague teases you about it, you may reply with a sarcastic, "Oh yes, this is scandalous! This would for sure be in the headlines tomorrow!" But if it's your strict boss who sternly calls you out on it, you would not be likely to make a sarcastic announcement in response.

Sarcasm is usually used to poke fun at someone or something and is heavily context and audience dependent. If you are around somebody who enjoys wit and has a sarcastic sense of humor, it will be quite welcome. Sarcasm is also dynamite when used to make a playful jab at yourself—the irony is how it can have the effect of making you seem supremely confident, self-aware and intelligent. Someone might say, "Oh no, I think I've lost that twenty dollars I was holding on to . . ." and you quickly jump in with, "Oh no! What an idiot. I would never do something so thoughtless. When *I* lose money, I make sure I lose the whole wallet and everything with it."

But around others who don't share the same sense of humor, are less secure, or don't like you, it's too easy for them to interpret your attempts at sarcastic humor as a full-fledged insult. That's not what you're aiming for here. They might just think that you are an insulting jackass, or they're more inclined to listen to the first part of the misdirection than the second.

Using misdirection in the wrong context will cause people to think you lack empathy or, worse, get your jollies from hurting other people's feelings. There will be others who simply won't get the sarcasm, no matter how obvious you make it. They won't be insulted, just very confused. You'll want to avoid both outcomes. The only way to do that is to make sure you "know your audience" and start small, judge the reaction you've had, and go from there. If other people happily use sarcasm themselves, it's probably a sign that they'll appreciate yours.

Choose the correct context and sarcasm can make you more likeable and charming. It also makes you look intelligent and witty. In some social circles, appropriate levels of sarcasm are not only welcomed, but required—think of it as a refreshing antidote to humble bragging or complaining.

Now that you have a clearer idea about the proper context of sarcasm, the next step is to articulate the elements to make sure you don't just insult people left and right in your attempts at building rapport. If your annoying coworker understood sarcasm better, they might be as funny as they think they are.

For the most part, **sarcasm is saying the *opposite* of (1) an objective fact, (2) a subjective emotion, or (3) thought.**

It makes a contradictory statement about a situation to either emphasize or downplay its effect.

Objective fact: Bob plays Tetris at work constantly.

Sarcastic statement: *Bob, you are the busiest man I know.*

Subjective emotion or thought: It is hilarious that Bob plays Tetris at work constantly.

Sarcastic statement: *Bob deserves a medal for worker of the year.*

Here's another one.

Objective fact: There is a surprising amount of traffic lately.

Sarcastic statement: *What are we going to do when we get to our destination super early?*

Subjective emotion or thought: I hate traffic so much.

Sarcastic statement: *This traffic is the best part of my day.*

That's the first and most common use of sarcasm. Now let's lay out a framework for different types of sarcasm and exactly when and how you can use it. You'll be surprised how formulaic and methodical you can get with this, and subsequently with humor.

When someone says or does something very obvious, you respond by saying something equally obvious.

Bob: "That road is very long."

You: "You are very observant."

Bob: "It's so hot today!"

You: "I see you're a meteorologist in training."

Poor Bob: "This menu is huge!"

You: "Glad to see you've learned to read!"

The next application of sarcasm is when something good or bad happens. You say something about how that good or bad event reflects on the other person.

If it's good, you say that it reflects badly on them; if it's bad, you say it reflects well on them.

Bob: "I dropped my coffee mug."

You: "You've always been so graceful."

Bob: "I got an F on my math test."

You: "Now I know who to call when my calculator breaks."

You observe Poor Bob dropping a cup of coffee and state "You would make a great baseball catcher. Great hands!"

Proper delivery is crucial for sarcasm. This can mean the difference between people laughing at your sarcastic joke, or thinking that you're serious in your sentiment and branding you an overall jerk. Also keep in mind that sarcasm is perhaps the most overused technique to create humor. Use it sparingly, but effectively.

You have to make it clear that you're being sarcastic and give others a sign indicating so. Otherwise, people will feel uncomfortable at the uncertainty. Are you just being mean, or are you trying to be funny?

The most common way to do this is with a combination of a deadpan vocal tone and a wry smile or smirk. With deadpan delivery, you don't laugh while you're saying it; you appear completely serious. Then, you break into a smile to alleviate the tension and clue others in to your true intention. If paired with a genuinely nonsensical or over-the-top statement, people will put two and two together and see what you've done.

Now that you know when to deliver sarcastic remarks, it's also important to learn about how to receive them and be a good audience. Let's pretend that you are Poor Bob from earlier and insert a reply for him.

Bob: "That road is very long."

You: "You are very observant."

Bob: "You know it. I'm like an eagle."

Bob: "It's so hot today!"

You: "I see you're a meteorologist in training."

Bob: "I can feel it in my bones. It's my destiny."

Poor Bob: "This menu is huge!"

You: "Glad to see you've learned to read!"

Redeemed Bob: **"I can also count to ten**."

You need to amplify their statement and what they are implying. Does this look familiar? It's a self-deprecating remark + a witty comeback! If you can volley back a sarcastic comment without even blinking, the humor is basically guaranteed. You'll appear sharp and quick, as well as confident enough to not be flustered by an off-color remark. In fact, you signal that you're game for some witty banter, and are happy to have a bit of fun in the conversation.

When you respond to sarcasm this way, it creates a greater bond. And just as important, you don't come off as a bad sport or someone who can't take a joke. Everybody is comfortable, and you create a funny situation and potential for greater banter. This is how so many long-standing in-jokes get their start in life. If you can remember one of these witty remarks and call back to it later in the conversation, congratulations, you now have a shared conversational history with the other person—and that can be a very powerful thing.

However, there is a downside when dealing with sarcasm. A lot of people who rely on sarcastic humor, pretty much on an automatic basis, are actually masking passive-aggressive personalities. They're constantly using sarcasm as a defense mechanism to hide their true feelings. They use sarcasm to pass off their otherwise negative emotions. They might be doing this to you, so it's important to know how to sidestep their subconsciously vicious attacks.

In such cases, responding with sarcasm will only encourage them. It indicates that misusing sarcasm in that way is acceptable. If you find someone being overly sarcastic with you in ways that are passive-aggressive, approach them and politely convey that their sarcasm feels hostile, even if they didn't intend it to be so. With sarcasm, it's all about *intention*. Are you laughing *at* or *with* someone? Who is the butt of the joke, if anyone?

Next, we have irony. Irony is a type of humor that is very close to sarcasm, and often confused with it.

Here's the official definition from Dictionary.com, just because it's something that people can struggle with nailing down: "the expression of one's meaning by using language that normally signifies the opposite, typically for humorous or emphatic effect."

This is different from sarcasm in a few ways. First, irony is generally about situations and incidents, not about people. Something happens which is the opposite of what you expected. When you're presented with an irony, like a fire station burning down, it will quite obviously be ironic, and not sarcastic. However, sarcasm is usually more derogatory in nature. You're saying things you don't mean. The definition of sarcasm is "the use of irony to mock or convey contempt." Thus, you can see how saying, "You are very observant," when someone says, "This road is very long," is sarcasm, not irony, because of the element of mockery inherent in the former remark. (Naturally, you'll be using sarcasm not to insult or convey contempt, but to create humor, which will hopefully build rapport and connection.)

Ironic humor is when something that is the exact opposite of what you might expect occurs. Another way to define irony is when you say something but mean the exact opposite of what you expect.

In other words, the words that come from your mouth are the opposite of the emotion you are feeling. If you're starving, an ironic statement might be something like, "I'm so full I need to unbuckle my belt. It's like

Thanksgiving in July."

Ironic humor draws its power from contrasts. There is a contrast between literal truth and perceived truth. In many cases, ironic humor stems from frustration or disappointment with our ideals. The way we imagine the world should be produces comedy when it clashes with how the world actually is.

Ironic humor is usually used to make a funny point about something or to point something out. For example, when you see a big a sign that says, "No signs allowed," that's ironic humor. The sign bans signs but is itself a sign. The expectation that the sign ensures there will be no signs in the vicinity failed.

Another example is when you see a car with a logo on the door saying, "Municipal Traffic Reduction Committee," and the car, along with everybody else, is stuck in two hours of bumper-to-bumper traffic. There is a profound ironic comedy there, as you would expect the traffic management planning committee would do a better job so they wouldn't be stuck in traffic themselves. It's like someone ordering a diet soda after they've just ordered three double cheeseburgers and fries or someone else crashing into a "thank you for not speeding" sign.

Irony is all about finding contrast and drawing some interesting and creative judgment out of it. As the examples indicate, ironic humor is more a matter of observation than one of spontaneity or creativity. You're more likely to find and point out things that are ironic than come up with something that is.

Ironic humor, on the other hand, is when you intentionally imply the opposite meaning of what you say. When we think about how to use irony conversationally, what we're really asking is what ways can we convey two messages at one time? So, your boss tells everyone to attend a meeting to discuss some issues with people being tardy to work and you slyly quip, "Sorry, Bev, is it all right if I'm ten minutes late?" with a big cheesy smile. (This, of course, depends on whether Bev is likely to find this funny or not . . .)

The Power of Improv

Let's turn our attention to a group of people who have made good banter and wit their business: improvisers and stand-up comedians.

The Rule of Improv Comedy: Great improv is a result of the creativity in spontaneous situations, and set agendas and outlines put a very low ceiling on that.

Improv comedy performances are, guess what, improvised!

The performers may occasionally work with a set theme that has been decided on beforehand, but there will always be large portions of an improv performance that involve taking direction from the crowd or audience. They can't predict what a crowd will give them to work with, so it's out of necessity that they can't have a strict agenda or outline.

That's part of the fun in attending an improv performance: you feel that you are a part of the outcome and have contributed to the show.

Obviously, these are situations where the performers have to think on their feet as quickly as possible, so they don't get tongue-tied and silent while everyone in the room is waiting. But overall, we have the perfect arena where we can watch spontaneity, curiosity, and good humor play out.

As an improv performer, you have to process what was said to you, try to project where you want the scene to go, and then predict what others might also say in response. And you have to do it all knowing that your plans might need to completely change when the other players switch things up. You have to read people's body language, try to determine if there is any ulterior message, and actively provide detail that other people can work with.

Improv comedy is collaborative in nature, but it's impossible to know what your teammates are thinking. In a split second, you need to perform a full analysis of the entire scene and spit out words that will enhance the most important aspects of it. Oh, and you're in front of a crowd of people, and there is a team of people on stage waiting on your response.

That might be the very definition of thinking on your feet (or hell on earth, if you're prone to anxiety!).

How does all of this make you a better conversationalist?

Recall that improv performances and conversations have the exact same goal—a flowing, entertaining interaction. If we look at some of the ways that improv performers are able to think fast and approach this unpredictability, we'll be able to improve our conversation skills immensely. *Without* trying too hard!

Don't Hold on Too Tightly

The first step, without a doubt, is to let go of any preconceived notion of how and where you want your conversation to go. Be "outcome independent." Professional improv players are able to create a fluid, dynamic, and witty interplay with their audience members because they are flexible and open to any possibility and direction. They are not stubborn or rigid—they understand that conversations *emerge* from the collaboration of the group and cannot be predicted or controlled too closely.

Yes, it can definitely be scary to go into a conversation with a completely blank slate, so to speak, especially if you are the type to plan and scheme. But planning and scheming has probably not gotten you too far in social conversations, so it's time to open up and let go of the talking points or agendas you want to take into your conversations with you.

Don't worry. I won't let you enter conversations unprepared—you just won't be using set agendas. By the way, when I mention set agendas, I mean goals, talking points, or objectives that people want to achieve or gain from a conversation. Your conversational resume? Sure. Your HPM and SBR tools? Absolutely. But these are temporary training wheels, and they're there to help natural conversation, not replace it.

When you talk to other people, the focus of the conversation should be about the conversation. Each conversation is its own animal, with its own inherent flow and natural rhythm. It should not be about you or what you are trying to get out of the other person or people. It shouldn't be forced to resemble a great conversation you've had before or some idea of how you think perfect conversations go. Why restrict yourself that way?

The moment other people are able to perceive your agenda, guess what happens? They will shut you out. You become somebody worthy of suspicion and skepticism. If you are trying to sell something, it makes it all that much harder once people feel that you have an ulterior motive. It's difficult to overcome the feeling that someone wants something from you. The same goes if you're trying to impress someone, to convince them of something, to get them to do this or that, to force them to pay attention to you. People want to feel like conversations are natural, fun, and something they do because they want to. Nobody wants to feel manipulated, right?

If you are approaching a conversation with an agenda, even an unconscious one, first it becomes exceedingly clear that you are only waiting for your turn to speak, and not actually listening to people. You aren't present and you aren't listening.

People might say something to you, and you might not even acknowledge their statement and just continue along with yours. You are telling them that you don't care about where the conversation is naturally heading—your agenda is more important. Others will notice your patterns sooner than you think. What are they getting out of a conversation like that?

Second, agendas leave people unready to adapt. Unless you are going to drop a speech on an audience, things will never go exactly as you plan.

When you create an agenda, you memorize it and become reliant on it. The more often that happens, the more uncomfortable we are with the unpredictability of thinking on our feet. You are essentially acting form fear—or reacting. What happens when you deviate and can't find a good place to step back into your agenda? You're left utterly unprepared for the rest of the interaction because of your reliance on what you've planned. You're no longer alive and authentic. You're like an actor on a stage who's forgotten their lines.

This is why it is extremely important to constantly listen to other people and acknowledge them. You might even go with *their* agenda. That's okay, because your goal here is to build rapport, and that will do it. Not holding on too tightly to an agenda sems scary until you realize that an agenda only gives you the illusion of control. That once you abandon it and just be in the moment, the real interesting stuff happens!

People can sometimes fall back on agendas or fixed plans out of fear or lack of confidence. They want to avoid that embarrassing moment when they're tongue-tied and awkward, unable to think of what to say next. But actually, it's those very moments that keep a conversation alive and interesting. And really, what's so wrong with finding yourself in an unexpected situation? Is it really the end of the world if you are not perfectly in control?

If you can trust yourself a little and surrender to the conversation rather than try to steer it, you give yourself opportunities to learn to become comfortable with that crucial moment, when all eyes are on you and it's time to say something. At the very least, don't underestimate the power of self-deprecating humor or a little disarming honesty:

Person A tells a witty joke, and you laugh, but suddenly feel at a loss for words and can't think of an equally funny thing to say. So, you shrug and say what you're really thinking: "You know, that's exactly the kind of brilliant joke that I could come up with, but you'll have to wait until three a.m. tomorrow morning for me to suddenly think of it…" In other words, you've made a witty joke… about not being able to make a witty joke. Congratulations, you've thought on your feet!

On the other hand, conversation is not about performance. If you can't think of anything to say, it's also a valid move to just pass the ball to someone else. Keep it going, whether all you do is ask a question, reiterate what's just happened, or use something unexpected to put the limelight back on someone else.

Learn to Make Quick Connections

Let people feel that the conversation is a two-way street. It actually becomes a two-way street when you stop, listen, and interrupt your own thoughts for theirs.

Up to this point in the chapter, we've discussed the negatives of over-preparing for conversations and coming in with outlines of what you want to discuss. Being able to rely solely on your ability to improvise is incredibly important, but just as frightening for some. So, how can we increase our capacity for quick thought?

There's no way other than through intentional practice. No, no rehearsing a script or churning out lines. But practice.

The first method is to turn on your favorite quick-witted television show with your remote in hand, because you'll be pausing constantly. For example, *30 Rock*, *Gilmore*

Girls, or even *Saturday Night Live*. These are all good shows to use because there is a lot of witty banter, and direct and indirect jokes. They have the type of dialogue we want to be able to create ourselves. (Actually, for our purposes, you don't even need to watch a show you find particularly funny. It's still useful just to watch how those jokes unfold, and how energy moves between the players).

Now, pretend that you are one of the characters on the screen. It doesn't matter who you are, as long as they have a lot of interaction with other characters. Then, when other characters reply to your character on screen, pause the show and construct your own reply. Play the show again and compare your responses. What do you notice? This is going to train your ability to think through different circumstances and come up with responses.

It's not going to be easy at first. You'll probably be blank a lot of the time and not know what to say. However, if you can do this for at least fifteen minutes a day for a week, you'll eventually become quicker with your replies. It'll start to feel more comfortable, even second nature. You can also practice this exercise with podcasts and radio interviews.

What you're doing is putting yourself in a position to think quickly. You can then hear what your character or avatar actually said, and you can get immediate feedback on what you could have said given the circumstances. You get to do all this at your own pace, and with the gift of being able to pause the conversation. Every piece of feedback is going to help hone your ability to come up with wit in record time.

The second method is to play free association with words and phrases. Free association is when you hear a word, then you come up with another word that the first word makes you think of. The second word can be anything, and the goal is to do this instantaneously.

For example, cat:dog, dog:puppy, puppy:paws, paws:fur, fur:allergies, allergies:medicine, medicine:nurses, nurses:doctors, doctors:plastic surgeon, plastic surgeon:fake lips, and so on. That was a free association word chain that began simply with the word cat.

How do you train this? Pick a word at random from a dictionary, and list out fifteen words in a free association word chain as quickly as possible. Then, do it again and again—

verbally, because that will require the quickest thinking. The trick here is not to try too hard. Don't think about it, literally just say what pops into your head, without censorship or mulling over it.

After you grow more comfortable with random free association with words, you can take the next step and choose two random words from a dictionary and pretend they are the name of a company. Then, create a short story about what that company does, as quickly as possible.

For example, the two random words you pick are: bottle, Africa. The short story I would construct about a company named "Africa Bottle" is that they import African homemade liquors. Sure, you'll probably come up with a few doozies as you practice this, but keep your judgment at bay—your only goal is to practice being swift and relaxed making associations.

The final step of this set of free association exercises is to choose five random words from the dictionary and make up a story that involves all of the words, as quickly as possible. Let's say you choose *hiccup, elevator, heat, president,* and *fern*. Then you quickly envisage a skit where the president once got overheated in an elevator in Hawaii and thus developed hiccups, which meant he had to postpone his media conference for ten minutes while one of the aides attempted to scare him again and again behind some fern bushes in the lobby. By showing him his latest approval ratings. In a way, this is not dissimilar from what you did with the R part of SBR, or the M part of HPM.

Again, these exercises train you to think quickly and be creative, so it's imperative that you do these exercises at "full speed," so you don't have the time to step in and start second-guessing yourself. They'll be tough, and at first, your responses might be terrible. But imagine how big the difference will be between your first day and your tenth day, for example. That's the power of free association, and practice.

If you also care to analyze the similarities between free association and conversation, you might find that they are virtually the same. In conversation, you'll reply to someone on a topic, a slightly related topic, or a new topic. That's exactly the type of thought process that free association takes. In a sense, you are training yourself to come up with conversation topics quickly. In another sense, you are training yourself to trust these first impulses and not self-censor—you may be surprised, in other words, at just how creative you can be when you simply get out of your own way!

The third method is to come up with a simple structure for yourself when you're backed into a corner. For example, an easy response structure you can use for just about anything is to (1) restate what was said, (2) state an emotion, and (3) ask a question.

Here's how that looks in practice:

"So, then I punched him in the face and all was well."

"You punched him in the face? That must have been satisfying. How did it feel after?"

"Did you like the coffee?"

"Did I like the coffee? Well, I'm in a great mood now, so I guess I did. What kind was it?"

"I hear the zoos here are amazing."

"The zoos are amazing? That would make me so happy to see one. Do you want to go tomorrow?"

It's an easy template that allows you to respond to anything, even if your mind is blank, because it literally tells you what to say. So, relax; even if you're in the pickliest of pickles, getting out of it can often be as simple as that. Skip a beat and don't sweat it—you'll be witty on the next one.

Have a Little Faith

What really makes confident people feel confident? So much of the beauty in our lives is unplanned. This occurs because we are able to step outside of the boxes and limits in our heads and explore things we wouldn't have otherwise. And what results is often amazing. Confidence could be called the belief in this truth.

Over-planning and preparing is like a straitjacket for your conversation and rapport. The irony is that holding things with lightness takes far less effort than trying to force and control them, and always leads to better results. In a way, it's about committing to having better conversations rather than becoming a better conversationalist—once you get your ego out of the picture, you can actually start to let things flow. But you have to take that first step, and that takes trust.

When you remove the possibility of spontaneity from your conversations, you might feel like you are safe from spectacular failure, but you also limit the potential of how high your conversation can soar. In other words, it's safe but boring.

The most memorable moments do not typically come because somebody planned them that way. In fact, it's usually the opposite.

Here's a quick thought experiment that will bolster your sense of confidence in the face of unpredictability. Hopefully it will help you realize that you don't need an agenda, and that your worst-case scenario is not really that bad.

Pick five topics that you know absolutely nothing about. Bring them up one by one with a friend. Commit to talking about each topic for at least five minutes. See the various angles and routes you can go to make a topic interesting. Grasp for straws on how to keep a dialogue going. Notably, see how you can relate it to other topics, and see how easy it is to get side-tracked onto something else. There's not much to fear, is there? You might convince yourself of something interesting: that the content of a conversation is only secondary, and your attitude and energy play a much, much bigger role.

The 1:1:1 Method of Storytelling

On the theme of simplifying storytelling, we've been talking about how we can use a mini story in many ways. You may be wondering what the difference is between a *mini* story and a *full-fledged* story.

To me, not much. As I mentioned, many people like to complicate storytelling as if they were composing an impromptu Greek tragedy. Does there have to be an introduction, middle, struggle, then resolution? You may have read that great stories are about X, Y, and Z; that you need a beginning, middle, and ending; that you should use as much descriptive detail as possible; or how important pauses are. That's one way of doing it, but certainly not the easiest or most practical.

My method of storytelling in conversation is to prioritize the discussion afterward—similar to what you saw with the fallback stories in an earlier chapter. This means that the story itself doesn't need to be that in-depth or long. It can and should contain specific details that people can relate to and latch on to, but it doesn't need to have parts or stages. It can be *mini* by nature. That's why it's called the *1:1:1 method*.

It stands for a story that (1) has one action, (2) can be summed up in one sentence, and (3) evokes one primary emotion in the listener. You can see why they're short and snappy. They also tend to make sure that you know your point before starting and have a very low chance of verbally wandering for minutes and alienating your listeners.

For a story to consist of *one action* means only one thing is happening. The story is about one occurrence. It should be direct and straightforward. Anything else just confuses the point and makes you liable to ramble.

A story should be able to be *summed up* in one sentence because, otherwise, you are trying to convey too much. This step actually takes practice, because you are forced to think about which aspects matter and which don't add anything to your action. It's a skill to be able to distill your thoughts into one sentence and still be thorough—often, you won't realize what you want to say unless you can do this.

Finally, a story should focus on one primary emotion to be evoked in the listener. And you should be able to name it! Keep in mind that evoking an emotion ensures that your story actually has a point, and it will color what details you carefully choose to emphasize that emotion. For our purposes here, there really aren't that many emotions you might want to evoke in others from a story. You might have humor, shock, awe, envy, happiness, anger, or annoyance. Those are the majority of reasons we relate our experiences to others.

Keep in mind that it's just my method for conveying my experiences to others. Whether people hear two sentences about a dog attack or they hear ten sentences doesn't change the impact of the story. The reason I abbreviate stories is so the conversation can move forward and we can then focus on the listener's impact and reaction. So what does this so-called story sound like?

"I was attacked by a dog and I was so frightened I nearly wet my pants." It's one sentence, there is one action, and the bit about wetting the pants is to emphasize the fact that the emotion you want to convey is fear and shock.

You could include more detail about the dog and the circumstances, but chances are people are going to ask about that immediately, so let them guide what they want to hear about your story. Invite them to participate! Very few people want to sit and listen to a monologue, most of which is told poorly and in a scattered manner. Therefore, keep the essentials but cut your story short, and let the conversation continue as a shared experience rather than you monopolizing the airspace. Make it a shared experience rather than all about you.

The 1:1:1 method can be summed up as starting a story as close to the end as possible. Most stories end before they get to the end, in terms of impact on the listener, their attention span, and the energy that you have to tell it. In other words, many stories tend to drone on because people try to adhere to these rules or because they simply lose the plot and are trying to find it again through talking. Above all else, a long preamble is not necessary. What's important is that people pay attention, care, and will react in some (preferably) emotional manner.

Ask for Stories

Most of the focus with stories is usually on telling them—but what about soliciting them from others and allowing them to feel as good as you do when a story lands well? What about stepping aside and giving other people the spotlight? Well, it's just a matter of how you ask for them.

When you watch sports, one of the most illogical parts is the post-game or post-match interview. These athletes are still caught in the throes of adrenaline, out of breath, and occasionally drip sweat on to the reporters.

Yet when you are watching a broadcaster interview an athlete, does anything odd strike you about the questions they ask? The interviewers are put into an impossible situation and usually walk away with decent soundbites—at the very least, not audio disasters. Their duty is to elicit a coherent answer from someone who is mentally incoherent at the moment. How do they do that?

They'll ask questions like: "So tell me about that moment in the second quarter. What did you feel about it and how did the coach turn it around then?" as opposed to: "How'd you guys win?" or: "How did you turn this match around, come back, and pull out all the stops to grab the victory at the very end?" as opposed to: "How was the comeback?"

The key? They ask for a story rather than an answer. They phrase their inquiry in a way that can only be answered with a story, in fact.

Detail, context, and boundaries are given for the athletes to set them up to talk as much as possible instead of providing a breathless one-word answer. It's almost as if they provide the athletes with an outline of what they want to hear and how they can proceed. They make it easy for them to tell a story and simply engage. It's like if someone asks you a question but, in the question, tells you exactly what they want to hear as hints.

Sometimes we think we are doing the heavy lifting in a conversation and the other party isn't giving us much to work with. But that's a massive cop-out. They might not be giving you much, but you also might be asking them the wrong questions, which is making them give you terrible responses. In fact, if you think you are shouldering the burden, you are definitely asking the wrong questions.

Conversation can be much more pleasant for everyone involved if you provide fertile ground for people to work in. Don't set the other person up to fail and be a poor conversationalist; that will only make you invest and care less and cause the conversation to die out.

When people ask me low-effort, vague questions, I know they probably aren't interested in the answer. They're just filling the time and silence. To create win-win conversations and better circumstances for all, ask for stories the way the sports broadcasters do. Ask questions in a way that makes people want to share.

Stories are personal, emotional, and compelling. There is a thought process and narrative that necessarily exists. They are what show your personality and are how you can learn about someone. They show people's emotions and how they think. Last but not least, they show what you care about.

Compare this with simply asking for closed-ended answers. Answers are often too boring and routine for people to care. They will still answer your questions but in a very literal way, and the level of engagement won't be there. Peppering people with shallow questions puts people in a position to fail conversationally.

It's the difference between asking, "What was the best part of your day so far? Tell me how you got that parking space so close!" instead of just, "How are you?"

When you ask somebody the second question, you're asking for a quick, uninvolved answer. You're being lazy and either don't care about their answer or want them to carry the conversational burden. When you ask somebody one of the first two questions, you're inviting them to tell a specific story about their day. You are inviting them to narrate the series of events that made their day great or not. And it can't really be answered with a one-word answer.

Another example is "What is the most exciting part of your job? How does it feel to make a difference like that?" instead of simply asking them the generic "What do you do?" When you only ask somebody what they do for a living, you know exactly how the rest of the conversation will go: "Oh, I do X. What about you?"

A final example is: "How did you feel about your weekend? What was the best part? It was so nice outside," instead of just: "How was your weekend?"

Prompting others for stories instead of simple answers gives them a chance to speak in such a way that they feel emotionally invested. This increases the sense of meaning they get from the conversation you're having with them. It also makes them feel you are genuinely interested in hearing their answer because your question doesn't sound generic.

Consider the following guidelines when asking a question:

1. Ask for a story
2. Be broad but with specific directions or prompts
3. Ask about feelings and emotions

4. Give the other person a direction to expand their answer into, and give them multiple prompts, hints, and possibilities
5. If all else fails, directly ask "Tell me the story about . . ."

Imagine that you want the other person to inform your curiosity. Other examples include the following:

1. "Tell me about the time you . . ." versus "How was that?"
2. "Did you like that . . ." versus "How was it?"
3. "You look focused. What happened in your morning . . ." versus "How are you?"

Let's think about what happens when you elicit (and provide) personal stories instead of the old, tired automatic replies.

You say hello to your co-worker on Monday morning and you ask how his weekend was. At this point, you have cataloged what you will say in case he asks you the same. Remember, they probably don't care about the actual answer ("good" or "okay"), but they *would* like to hear something interesting. But you never get the chance, because you ask him "How was your weekend? Tell me about the most interesting part—I know you didn't just watch a movie at home!"

He opens up and begins to tell you about his Saturday night when he separately and involuntarily visited a strip joint, a funeral, and a child's birthday party. That's a conversation that can take off and get interesting, and you've successfully bypassed the unnecessary and boring small talk that plagues so many of us.

Most people love talking about themselves. Use this fact to your advantage. Once someone takes your cue and starts sharing a story, make sure you are aware of how you're responding to that person through your facial expressions, gestures, body language, and other nonverbal signals. Since there is always at least one exciting thing in any story, focus on that exciting point and don't be afraid to show that you're engaged.

One quick tip to show that you're engaged and even willing to add is something I call *pinning the tail on the donkey*. There is probably a better name for it, but my vocabulary was severely lacking at the time. The donkey is the story from someone else, while the tail is your addition to it. It allows you to feel like you're contributing, it makes other people know you're listening, and it turns into something you've created together.

People will actually love you for it because, when you do this, your mindset becomes focused on assisting people's stories and letting them have the floor.

Bob's story: "I went to the bank and tripped and spilled all my cash, making it rain inadvertently."

Tail: **"Did you think you were Scrooge McDuck for a second?"**

When you make a tail, try to home in on the primary emotion the story was conveying, then add a comment that amplifies it. The story was about how Bob felt rich, and Scrooge McDuck is a duck who swims in pools of gold doubloons, so it adds to the story and doesn't steal Bob's thunder. Get into the habit of assisting other people's stories. It's easy, witty, and extremely likable because you are helping them out.

Conversational diversity

Hypotheticals

A hypothetical is a classic conversational diversification tactic. Okay, that's a fancy term for what really amounts to, "Hey, what would you do if . . ." and "What do you think about . . ."

But here's what happens when you throw a hypothetical into your conversation. You inject exponentially the amount of variability and unpredictability possible because it's likely something your conversation partner has never considered, and the hypothetical you pose will be something that has no clear or correct answer. Instead, something hopefully exciting comes out of it and you get to discuss something that would never have come up otherwise.

Use hypotheticals to see how people react and how their minds work. You'll learn something about them from how they answer, and you can treat the hypothetical itself like an inkblot test—how they answer probably says something about them. In the end, wherever it goes will probably be more interesting than an interview!

The easiest way to make a conversation awkward or to introduce dead space is to ask questions that can easily be answered by a simple yes or no. Open-ended questions allow for creativity. They allow people to dig into their memory banks, come up with random associations, or otherwise trigger their imagination. With that said, your hypothetical question should be challenging enough so that the recipient actually needs to be a bit creative in answering the question.

The secret to hypotheticals is to make them appear spontaneous. Ask for their opinion on something out of curiosity. You don't want to come off as contrived or like you're reading from a script. That's going to make you look ingenuous. And you don't want to seem as if you have some sort of agenda.

Adding a one- to two-sentence backstory as to why this thought "spontaneously" popped into your mind tends to help.

Finally, keep in mind that when you use these, you must also have an answer prepared for the hypothetical you ask. You can step in with your answer while they are formulating theirs—and you should have thought about this answer beforehand so you can be prepared and rehearse it. Don't be in a situation where you don't know the answer to your own hypothetical. You don't need a definitive answer, but you at least need a stance or opinion. There's nothing worse than your conversation partner saying, "I don't know," and you also saying, "I don't know." Nothing else will fill that space besides awkward silence.

Here are some examples of hypothetical questions you can toss into your conversations like a grenade. It's a good rule of thumb to have a few prepared and up your sleeve for when you sense you are falling into some type of routine or pattern.

Type #1: What would you do if . . .

Example: What would you do if the waiter from lunch screamed at you to give him a bigger tip?

Type #2: Would you rather have this or that?

Example: Would you rather be four inches shorter or sixteen inches taller?

Type #3: My friend just did/said this . . . What would you have done?

Example: My friend just called out his boss for working too much. Can you imagine that? What would you have done?

Type #4: What if you were in this situation . . .?

Example: What if your co-worker was stealing your food from the fridge every day? How would you handle that?

Type #5: Which of the following . . .?

Example: Which do you think is better: super cold winters or hot summers?

Type #6: Who do you think . . .?

Example: Which of us do you think got the best grades in school? Or the worst?

Think Out Loud

This is a rather simplistic way of phrasing it, but thinking out loud can introduce quite a bit of conversational diversity. We filter ourselves far too much, and while it's called for sometimes, it doesn't always help.

If we just voice our inner monologue about what we're thinking about during our day, this can be quite an icebreaker. Share your thoughts about your surroundings or what you observe around you. Share what you are doing, what you are seeing, what you are thinking, and what you are wondering. Thinking out loud can also just be voicing your feelings, such as, "I'm so happy with the sunshine right now," or, "I can't believe the coffee here is so expensive!"

This will lead to a more open flow of communication. Others will feel less guarded around you and that can lead to a higher level a mutual comfort. It's also bound to be more interesting than filling the silence with a question that no one cares about.

Just say what's on your mind and you are inviting others to speak, but it's not a demand.

The added benefit is you'll probably end up being that person who says what everyone is thinking but is afraid to say. Maybe they're just shy or want to seem polite. Whatever it is, they are thinking it, but they feel it's not proper to voice their thoughts aloud. If you become that person who is the first to say what everyone is thinking, you break the ice.

People will feel they can trust you and be comfortable around you because you actually have the guts to say what they wanted to say. At least you'll bring up some common ground that others can comment on.

Summary

- Lightness, humor and playfulness are the life blood of good conversation, and there are ways to develop them for yourself.
- One quick technique is misdirection, where a statement has two parts: the first

is expected and ordinary, the second contradicts it with unexpected and comedic results. Sarcasm can be powerful but is best when directed at yourself and used with those you are more familiar with. Ironic humor is similar to sarcasm, but more focused on the observation of the contrast between the expected and the actual.

- The world of improv has a lot to teach us about good conversational chemistry. One improv rule is not to hold on to any outcome too tightly, and be ready to follow the emerging flow of the conversation.

- Another rule is to rely on quick connections to make sure you always have something to say. This can be practiced by free associating one, two, or five words. Good improv is about having faith in the conversation's direction, and your ability to be okay with where it goes.

- The 1:1:1 method of storytelling is a mini story technique that relies on one action, summarized in one sentence, that evokes one main emotion in the listener. This keeps your stories engaging, short, and effective. Alternatively, you can ask for other people's stories.

- Conversational diversity is about having as many different tools in your toolkit as possible. Hypothetical questions are one such tool. These kinds of "what if . . .?" questions inject some excitement, creativity, and unpredictability, while showing something interesting about the person giving the answer.

- Finally, thinking out loud can be a way to turn monologues into dialogues. If we speak freely and without self-censoring, we break the ice, share ourselves honestly, and invite (rather than demand) others to join us.

Summary Guide

CHAPTER 1: SO, WHAT IS CHARISMA ANYWAY?

- Charming people may seem to possess a mysterious quality nobody else does, but charisma is a knowable set of social and emotional behaviors that anyone can learn.
- Charisma can be defined as a blend of likeability and influence. Charismatics have presence in a room, can impact and persuade others, can lead, but also know how to put people at ease, are warm, smile often, and get along with anyone.
- Practice taking up more space in a room, and examine any core beliefs that may negatively impact your posture and expression. Believe deep down that other people are not a threat and that you have something worthwhile to communicate.
- Speak openly about your passions, and when you address others, speak to their highest selves. Smile often and remember the details of what people tell you.

- Don't interrupt, judge, complain, gossip or express negativity. Instead, express gratitude and optimism.
- Ronald Riggio broke charisma into 3 social and emotional functions: expressiveness, sensitivity to other people's expressiveness, and self-control.
- To be more charismatic, express yourself emotionally with colorful language and dynamic facial expressions. Pay attention to people's nonverbal expression, but don't be afraid to ask directly about how others feel.
- To improve emotional control, slow down, breathe and become present, rather than reacting mindlessly.
- Acting and improv can help you improve social skills, and the ability to consciously wear a social mask. Pay attention to how you're physically presenting yourself and dress with care and deliberation.
- Finally, learn to "people watch" and get into the habit of asking more questions instead of talking about yourself in conversations.

CHAPTER 2: BUILDING REAL-WORLD CHARISMA

- Olivia Fox Cabane explains how there are four charisma types according to the proportion of power, presence and warmth. The focused charismatic (who pays deep attention to others), the visionary charismatic (who communicates their infectious passion), the kind charismatic (who inspires with warmth and compassion) and the authoritative charismatic (who leads others with expertise and power).
- Depending on your goals, you can play up your natural charisma strengths or seek to balance out your weaknesses.
- To be socially and emotionally comfortable, plan ahead and make sure you're physically comfortable, which will remove barriers to charismatic connection.
- Use ritual and visualization as a "social warm up." Music, meditation, and affirmations can help you prepare.
- Build presence with mindfulness. Slow down, breathe and anchor in the senses. Pause before you respond, and take conscious care of every detail of the interaction, including your verbal and nonverbal expression, appearance, and behavior.

- Howard Friedman emphasized the affective, nonverbal expressiveness component of charisma.
- Communicate with *all* your body and laugh openly. Speak with a dynamic, varied voice that changes in pitch, tone and expression. Use touch to bridge distance and create warmth, aware that the rules differ for men and women.
- Speak less and emote more via facial expression. If you find yourself the center of attention, relax and don't draw attention to awkwardness, using humor to defuse tension. Use exaggerated, pantomime-like gestures and initiate contact with strangers. Finally, practice the art of "platonic flirting."
- Introverts *can* be charismatic, but they must do so on their own terms.

CHAPTER 3: PUTTING IT ALL TOGETHER

- We can condense the four theories of charisma into 5 distinct charismatic traits: likeability and warmth; power and influence; emotional intelligence; presence, awareness and self-control; and social intelligence and leadership. If we can consistently hit these five notes in our social interactions, we cannot help but boost our "charisma quotient."

- To be impactful, charisma has to be genuine to us. We need to take responsibility for honestly appraising our skills and taking concrete action to improve in real life. Whether we are extroverted or introverted, there is a unique charisma style that will work for us.

- Real life celebrities and historical figures can serve as examples and inspiration. Both Will Smith and Marilyn Monroe show how you can tick all 5 charisma boxes, but in completely different ways.

- Will Smith teaches us to be prepared, stay humble and work hard, and lead with positivity, humor, and good-naturedness. Though his social mask makes him appear easygoing and lighthearted, it conceals the effort, deliberation and hard work required to build the life and image you want.

- Marilyn Monroe teaches us that charisma can also be about magnetically drawing people towards you, rather than being loud and over the top to demand attention. Marilyn shows us the power of appearance, and how to craft a performing person down to the finest detail. She also shows us indirectly that perfection is not required, and that if you can lean honestly into your own vulnerability and fragility, people may love you all the more for it.

- You can design your own unique charisma formula by honestly rating how you perform in each of these five areas, and committing to taking action today to improve.

CHAPTER 4: THE BEDROCK OF GOOD COMMUNICATION

- Part 1 of this book is all about the charismatic presence. How might you wish for someone to describe you, and how much does that differ from reality? And then, how do you bridge the gap between these two versions of yourself? Part 1 is more theoretical and introspective, while Part 2 is all about action. How do you actually create the type of interactions that will draw people to you, regardless of your current personality?
- Unsurprisingly, it all starts with empathy. When you have empathy, you know what other people are thinking and feeling, or at least you can make a pretty darned good

guess about it. And if we know what people are thinking and feeling, we can also make a darned good guess as to what they want. And that's what will allow us to create charismatic interactions.

- The first is to simply read more. This is probably the best practice you can do without having someone in front of you, because it forces you to inhabit someone else's perspective and inner dialogue. You can see in the story that because X happened, Y and Z might happen. This seems simple, but it is not easy to practice in daily life. Having an experience filter is very similar, in that it forces you to step out of your perspective (which is necessarily limited) and really try to see someone else's. It might sound like we are only talking about empathy here, but the truth is that empathy and charisma are extremely, extremely related. Yes, deliberately practicing theory of mind is also more in the same direction of understanding another person's thoughts and emotions.

- Finally, understanding the difference between facts and interpretation will help you know what you should respond to. Almost always, you should be trying to respond to people's interpretation because their emotions are buried within, and that's what will draw people to you.

CHAPTER 5: ENGAGING FULLY

- In order to interact and engage more fully in conversations, we need to work against our not-so-useful habits and learn better ones.
- A non-negotiable habit is becoming a master at using questions. The right questions help people feel closer to us, communicate our attention and care, share our competence, show that we're aware and paying attention, deepen intimacy, guide the conversation, and make us more trustworthy.
- All exchanges, and hence all questions, are typically on one of three possible levels: those exchanging factual information, those exchanging feelings and emotions, and those communicating deeper values. In social situations, you'll lean more heavily on the last two, but a good conversation works when people have similar conversational goals and are matched in the level they're interacting on.
- Conversational narcissism is an impediment to curiosity, engagement, and

good question asking. Whether unconscious or conscious, this usually results from us placing something other than connection with the other person as our goal for conversation, i.e. to brag, to defend, to compete.

- We can reduce our own conversational narcissism by using questions. Follow-up questions are very effective, as are open-ended questions that don't make people uncomfortable, but may *gently* push on the barrier or normal etiquette.

- Just as a role model can be a guide and inspiration for your own behavior, a model can also help you stay curious when you talk to others. Talk show hosts are experts and placing their conversation partners front and center, so we can ask, what would they do? Usually, the answer is "treat my guest like the most interesting person in the whole universe."

- Curiosity needs to be genuine. We all have a bias against others sometimes, assuming they're not very interesting, but unless we ask, we won't learn about their more fascinating sides. Assume that everyone has something to teach you, and foster a genuine inquisitiveness into the details of their world. I guarantee you will not be disappointed.

CHAPTER 6: SUBTLY CHARISMATIC

- Lightness, humor and playfulness are the life blood of good conversation, and there are ways to develop them for yourself.

- One quick technique is misdirection, where a statement has two parts: the first is expected and ordinary, the second contradicts it with unexpected and comedic results. Sarcasm can be powerful but is best when directed at yourself and used with those you are more familiar with. Ironic humor is similar to sarcasm, but more focused on the observation of the contrast between the expected and the actual.

- The world of improv has a lot to teach us about good conversational chemistry. One improv rule is not to hold on to any outcome too tightly, and be ready to follow the emerging flow of the conversation.

- Another rule is to rely on quick connections to make sure you always have something to say. This can be practiced by free associating one, two, or five words. Good improv is about having faith in the conversation's direction, and your ability to be okay with where it goes.

- The 1:1:1 method of storytelling is a mini story technique that relies on one action, summarized in one sentence, that evokes one main emotion in the listener. This keeps your stories engaging, short, and effective. Alternatively, you can ask for other people's stories.
- Conversational diversity is about having as many different tools in your toolkit as possible. Hypothetical questions are one such tool. These kinds of "what if . . .?" questions inject some excitement, creativity, and unpredictability, while showing something interesting about the person giving the answer.
- Finally, thinking out loud can be a way to turn monologues into dialogues. If we speak freely and without self-censoring, we break the ice, share ourselves honestly, and invite (rather than demand) others to join us.